FOOD STORAGE MADE EASY

a three-part program

Checklists * Encyclopedia * Recipes

by Jodi Moore and Julie Weiss

Jodi and Julie - Food Storage Made Easy
P.O. Box 1105
Riverton Utah, 84064

A Note from Jodi and Julie

We are so excited that you decided to purchase this book about food storage! If you are a food storage veteran, we appreciate you adding our book as another resource for you. If you are new to food storage ... you have just taken the first step in your food storage and preparedness journey which you may discover is not as scary, hard, or boring as you thought it would be. We wanted to introduce ourselves and let you know a little about how this book came about and how to best use it. We are Jodi and Julie, two busy moms, and we will be your tour guide through this exciting new adventure.

Confession time: Our journey began eight years ago when we had zero food storage, tight budgets, a burning desire to help our growing little families to be prepared, and no clue how to get started. We didn't even know what wheat looked like ... let alone how to use it. This book is the result of our own personal journey of discovery. We developed checklists, food calculators, homemade #10 stoves, rotating can racks made of cardboard, and many other tools that helped us get more prepared and compiled all of our learnings into this three-part program.

In this book we will walk you through a process that will save you time, money, and mistakes as you build your food storage. If you follow our plan you will have a complete family preparedness plan, 72 hour kits, a car emergency kit, an emergency binder, water storage, a year supply of food, and all of the tools, recipes, and knowledge needed to actually use your food storage should an emergency situation arise.

We excited for you to be able to use this book as a resource. Share it with your family and friends because it is always more fun to work on these things with a buddy. And most importantly we hope that we can help make your own food storage journey a little more EASY!

-Jodi and Julie

HOW TO USE THIS BOOK:

Part One: Checklists - Follow each checklist at your own pace according to your time and financial situation. You will be given assignments to purchase, to do/learn, and recipes to try using the items you will be purchasing.

Part Two: Food Storage Encyclopedia - Each checklist will refer you to specific articles located in the encyclopedia to learn about food options, tutorials, calculators, and more. This section is formatted as a series of ten BabySteps plus a substantial section on emergency preparedness. While it was created to accompany the checklists, it can also be read straight through to get a great overview of general food storage principles.

Part Three: Recipe Appendix - All the recipes referred to in the checklists can be found in this section. These are tried and true recipes that we have discovered or created ourselves. They are kid- friendly and can be used in your everyday cooking to help with food rotation and to get you used to cooking and eating your food storage foods.

Part One: Checklists

Part Two: Food Storage Encyclopedia

BABYSTEP 7: BAKING INGREDIENTS

BABYSTEP 8: FRUITS AND VEGGIES

BABYSTEP 9: COMFORT FOODS

BABYSTEP 10: NON-FOOD ITEMS

Part Three: Recipe Appendix

RECIPES:

CHECKLISTS

These checklists were developed to help spread purchases for your food storage throughout an entire year. They contain to-do lists that help you learn about and actually use your food storage. We recommend going through one checklist every two weeks.

Each checklist has three sections. The sections are:

- **TO PURCHASE:** The items listed to purchase in the checklists will provide enough food, water, and supplies for one adult for one year. These items can often be found online. Amazon has great prices on tools and appliances, Costco offers some great food storage packages, and all of the big brands of food have online stores you can shop at if you don't have a local source.

- **TO DO:** The articles that you will be instructed to read are found in the corresponding sections of the Food Storage Made Easy Encyclopedia, and will be underlined in the bullet points.

- **RECIPES TO TRY:** The recipes you will be trying out can all be found in the Recipe Appendix. If there isn't a recipe to try, this section will not be on the checklist.

Checklist Recommendations Explained

The amounts given in the checklists will buy a one year supply of food for one adult. Please modify how much you purchase to fit your budget, your family size, and your goals. Some people decide their goal for the first year is to accumulate a 3 month supply for their entire family. Remember, it is not recommended to go into debt to build your food storage.

The items assigned to purchase include foods from the standard (life-sustaining) Long Term Calculator, along with a few extra items. These extra items will greatly enrich your food storage, give you more variety, and help you avoid diet fatigue if you are using it for an extended amount of time. The extra items will be for you to try, and then decide if you would like to store more of them.

Life Sustaining Long Term Calculator Foods:
Grains, Fats and Oils, Legumes, Sugars, Milk, Cooking Essentials

Extra Items to Enrich your Food Storage:
Dairy Powders (Butter and Sour Cream), Egg Powders, Dehydrated Fruits and Vegetables, Freeze-Dried Fruits and Vegetables, Freeze-Dried Meats, Gluten, Freeze-Dried Cheeses, Frozen and Canned Fruits and Vegetables

We are so excited that you have made the commitment to get your food storage in order this year! There are many reasons WHY people build a Food Storage. Whatever your reasons, we are here to help you along the way.

This week's focus: Emergency Preparedness

We recommend people get a basic Emergency Plan in place before they really dive into their food storage program. If you have a 72 hour kit of food, water, and supplies you will be better off in an emergency than 95% of the country. This list may feel daunting, so feel free to spread out the tasks over more than two weeks if you need to.

For this checklist we will be working on the Emergency Preparedness Plan {found on page 38}. The tasks will cover the three areas of our Emergency Preparedness Plan:

- Family Plan
- Disaster Kit (includes 72 hour kits and emergency binder)
- Evacuation List (includes evacuation list, car kit, and computer backup)

TO DO:

✓ Read Why Food Storage {found on page 36}

✓ Read Emergency Preparedness Introduction {found on page 37}

✓ Fill out the Emergency Preparedness Plan and use it as a step-by-step guide to complete the following tasks: {found on pages 38-47}

- Fill out the Family Plan section and go over it with your family
- Inventory and gather supplies you have on hand for your Disaster Kits
- Follow instructions to create your own Emergency Binder
- Fill out your Evacuation List in order of priority
- Inventory and gather supplies you have on hand for your Car Kits

✓ Read and create an Emergency Kits For Babies if applicable {found on page 54}

TO PURCHASE:

✓ Food, water, and cooking tools for 72 Hour Kits and other Disaster Kit supplies

✓ Supplies needed to create your Emergency Binder

✓ Remaining supplies needed for Car Kits

✓ Supplies or online services to back-up your computers

For this checklist we will focus on preparing your space to make room for all of the great food storage items you will be buying. It feels so much more doable to get started if you know you have a good location picked out and the shelf space readily available.

This week's focus: BabyStep 1

People often put off starting a food storage because they don't feel like they have enough space to store it all. We have come up with some great tips to help overcome this hurdle. We also have plans available to create your own inexpensive shelves if you don't have the money for a comprehensive can rotation system just yet.

TO PURCHASE:

✓ Purchase one of these shelf options that meets your storage needs:
  • Inexpensive metal or plastic shelving
  • Higher quality metal shelves (the Gorilla shelves from Costco are great)
  • Pantry Organizer Rotating Racks (from Thrive Life)

✓ Purchase or build rotating racks to keep your smaller cans organized:
  • Build cardboard racks using boxes and glue using our tutorial {found on page 66}
  • Purchase cardboard CanOrganizers (cheap and convenient)
  • Purchase plastic CanSolidators (durable and customizable)

TO DO:

✓ Clean out an area for your food storage, create a space that makes you feel motivated!

✓ Before buying your shelf, decide what type of system will work best for your individual needs. Read BabyStep 1 Introduction {found on page 60}

✓ As you create your storage space, consider future needs for growth and how you will store your foods. Read Can and Bucket Storage {found on page 68}

✓ For creative space ideas read Small Space Storage Solutions {found on page 61}

✓ Build your shelves or cardboard racks using our tutorial depending on which options you chose for your shelving solutions {found on page 66}

For this checklist we are going to be working on our water storage which is one of the most important aspects of food storage. You can live for weeks without food, but only a few days without water. There are many different recommendations for the amount of water to store. A general guideline to follow is to store 1 gallon per person for 3-14 days for drinking. Three days should be the bare minimum, and plan to store extra for cleaning, cooking, etc.

This week's focus: BabyStep 2

Water is difficult to store in large quantities and yet it is necessary to have access to a lot of it in a true emergency situation. Typically disaster aid organizations are able to make it into affected areas within 3 days, thus the 3 day minimum typically recommended. However, it is always good to have some backup plans in place for how you would deal with an extended water shortage situation. Start with the basics of water storage and move on to the more advanced topics over time.

TO PURCHASE:

✓ Purchase or collect water storage containers {options found on page 70}
  • Use sterilized 2 liter pop or juice bottles, or any size store-bought water bottles
  • Small mylar pouches or water cartons
  • 5/6 gallon plastic jugs, water box kits, or waterbricks
  • Water barrels

✓ Purchase purification/filtration products
  • Bleach or water treatment drops
  • Water filtration bottles or straws
  • SteriPens

✓ Purchase some drink mixes to help improve the taste of stored water
  • Kool-Aid, fruit drink mixes, cocoa, tang, etc. are all options

TO DO:

✓ Fill your water containers and store them in a couple different areas in your home
  • Don't forget to add some bleach or other purification additive

✓ Study up on water storage. Read the following:
  • <u>BabyStep 2 Introduction</u> {found on page 69}
  • <u>Water Storage Containers</u> {found on page 70}
  • <u>Water Rotation and Conservation</u> {found on page 73}
  • <u>Water Filtration Vs Purification</u> {found on page 75}

We are going to be BUSY as we work through this checklist. We will be going into some intense detail on how to plan and purchase your Three Month Food Supply. This may sound intimidating but it is actually fun to do! Once you have your initial plan in place the rest of the process is not difficult at all.

This week's focus: BabyStep 3

Planning your Three Month Supply is very important for your preparedness plans. If you had a tight month financially, wouldn't it be great to know that you could at least cut on grocery costs and still feed your family the foods they are used to? Some people plan for only shelf stable meals (using only pantry items), while others opt to include some freezer foods as well. Determine which type of meals you feel are right for your family and make your plan based off of those meals.

TO PURCHASE:

✓ Begin purchasing foods included on your 3 Month Food Supply list once you have your plan of what you would like to purchase
  • Use a service like Deals to Meals to save you money on these purchases

TO DO:

✓ Create your three month food supply plan
  • Read BabyStep 3 Introduction {found on page 76}
  • Read 3 Month Supply Planning: Questions To Ask Yourself {found on page 77}
  • Read 3 Month Supply Planning {found on page 78}
  • Fill out your Menu Plan or Excel Worksheet. Photocopy additional sheets as necessary {found on pages 79-80}
  • Place your completed plan worksheets where they will remind you to keep using and rotating your foods on a regular basis
  • Update your inventory sheet of what foods you already have stored

✓ Find or develop some shelf stable recipes if you opt to use these in your planning
  • The included Recipe Appendix has good shelf stable options {found on page 138}

✓ Develop a system for purchasing your food items that works for your shopping style
  • Buy a few extras of several items each time you grocery shop
  • Stock up on items when they are on sale
  • Learn more about coupon shopping

Now that you have your Three Month Supply worksheet filled out we are going to give you a reminder in each checklist to continue to stock up and replenish your supply. This should be incorporated into your normal grocery budget (especially if you are taking advantage of sales and coupons). For this checklist we will be introducing you to the world of long term food storage.

This week's focus: BabyStep 4

Let's talk about long term food storage a little more in depth. For the rest of the checklists we will give you specific purchasing assignments for items which are included in our food storage calculator. The food storage calculator contains life sustaining foods. In addition to the life-sustaining foods, we recommend storing some other items that will enrich your food storage as well as some critical non-food items. For a complete outline of what the purchasing assignments are made up of, see the introduction to the checklists {found on page 8}. The amounts indicated to purchase in the checklists are to provide a 1 year supply for 1 adult.

TO PURCHASE:

✓ Purchase some food storage cookbooks to start getting ideas on what to cook

✓ Purchase something from your 3 month supply list, remember to update your list
  • Stock up on sale items, buy some things in bulk, or pick up a few extras items

TO DO:

✓ Familiarize yourself with your Long Term Food Storage plan and make your goals
  • Read BabyStep 4 Introduction {found on page 81}
  • Read Long Term Storage Planning {found on page 83}
  • Look over the Long Term Storage Calculator {found on pages 84-85}

✓ Refer to Food Storage Shelf Life as you make a rotation plan {found on pages 86-87}

✓ Read Food Storage Myths {found on page 82}

✓ Inventory what foods you already have stored {use calculator on pages 84-85}

✓ Before packaging any of your food read Oxygen Absorbers {found on page 88}

✓ For alternatives to our calculator read Healthy Food Storage {found on page 90}

The first long term food storage item we will cover is grains which is BabyStep 5. Wheat is the most commonly stored grain so we'll be learning to use it first. For this checklist we will be learning about, purchasing, and actually cooking with wheat. We will also start buying items from your non-food items list in each checklist which is BabyStep 10.

This week's focus: BabySteps 5 & 10

People often wonder why wheat is such a big staple in the world of food storage. The answer is simple, if you store wheat and just a few other basic cooking ingredients you can make a wide variety of foods such as breads, tortillas, wheat grass, pasta, cakes, puddings, cookies, waffles, biscuits, muffins, crackers, and more! Not only that but wheat is inexpensive, has a long shelf life, and is extremely healthy, it's definitely the "staff of life".

TO PURCHASE:

✓ Purchase 50 lbs of wheat

✓ Purchase a 6 month supply of toilet paper
  • To determine quantities, measure usage for a week and then multiply by 26

✓ Purchase something from your 3 month supply list, remember to update your list
  • Stock up on sale items, buy some things in bulk, or pick up a few extras items

TO DO:

✓ Read <u>BabyStep 5 Introduction</u> {found on page 91}

✓ Read <u>BabyStep 10 Introduction</u> {found on page 134} for an overview on grains and non-food items

✓ Read <u>All About Wheat</u> to learn about wheat {found on page 92}

✓ Read <u>Food Storage and Allergies</u> and update your calculator to include grains you can tolerate if you are allergic to wheat {found on page 89}

✓ Read <u>Using Wheat Without a Wheat Grinder</u> {found on page 102}

✓ Read <u>All About Grain Mills</u> and start saving up for a grain mill {found on page 97}

RECIPES TO TRY:

❖ Whole Wheat Pizza Dough (use whole wheat flour) {found on page 168}
❖ Blender Wheat Pancakes (no grinder required) {found on page 144}

Hopefully you are now more comfortable using your wheat. Now we are going to give you a new food to try ... legumes! The legumes category includes dried beans, lentils, soy beans, split peas, lima beans, and dry soup mixes. We will start with purchasing dried beans and also start assigning baking ingredients throughout future checklists.

This week's focus: BabySteps 6 & 7

Dried beans are an excellent item for food storage because they are inexpensive, a great source of fiber and protein, have a long storage life, and are very versatile. Once you learn how to use them you will find ways to use beans very often in your everyday cooking. You can use mashed up beans to replace the butter or oil in recipes. Start out with a few different varieties of beans until you learn the kinds your family likes best.

TO PURCHASE:

✓ Purchase 25 lbs of dried beans (choose a combination of your favorite kinds)

✓ Purchase 4 lbs of shortening or shortening powder

✓ Purchase 1 qt of salad dressing

✓ Purchase a few extra boxes of laundry detergent

✓ Purchase something from your 3 month supply list, remember to update your list
  • Stock up on sale items, buy some things in bulk, or pick up a few extras items

TO DO:

✓ Read <u>BabyStep 6 Introduction</u> {found on page 103}

✓ Read <u>All About Baking Ingredients: Fats and Oils Section</u> {found on page 113}

✓ Read <u>All About Dried Beans</u> {found on page 104}

✓ Research pressure cookers to determine if you want to buy one

RECIPES TO TRY:

❖ Real Chili Beans {found on page 163}
❖ Cookie Recipe (try a family favorite and replace the fat with beans}
❖ Salsa, Chicken, and Black Bean Soup {found on page 164}
❖ Homemade Hummus (uses garbanzo beans) {found on page 155}
❖ Homemade Ranch Dressing (if not storing salad dressing) {found on page 156}

For this checklist we are going to be learning details about powdered milk including how much to buy, what kind to buy, and how to use it. We will also be introducing you to comfort foods and encouraging you to start buying some.

This week's focus: BabyStep 7 & 9

Different food calculators will have different recommendations for the amounts to store. Our recommendations are a general guideline, if you have small children or a pregnant/nursing mother in the home you may want to increase the amount of milk that you store. It's also important to note that the purchase amounts listed are for non-instant dry milk. If you choose to store Instant Milk instead you will need to double the amount you buy since it is less concentrated than regular dry milk.

TO PURCHASE:

✓ Purchase 8 lbs of non-instant dry milk (double this amount if storing instant dry milk)

✓ Purchase 3 lbs of honey or honey crystals

✓ Purchase some of your favorite comfort foods to add to your storage

✓ Purchase something from your 3 month supply list, remember to update your list
  • Stock up on sale items, buy some things in bulk, or pick up a few extras items

TO DO:

✓ Read <u>All About Baking Ingredients: Sugars Section</u> {found on page 114}

✓ Read <u>BabyStep 9 Introduction</u> {found on page 132}

✓ Read <u>All About Powdered Milk</u> {found on page 115}

✓ Read <u>All About Honey</u> {found on page 117}

✓ Replace the regular milk in at least ONE of your baking recipes with powdered milk

✓ Refer to <u>Food Storage Equivalents Chart</u> as needed {found on page 140}

RECIPES TO TRY:

❖ Honey Whole Wheat Bread (use powdered milk and honey) {found on page 158}
❖ Super Cherry Pie (use homemade sweetened condensed milk) {found on page 165}
❖ Hot Fudge Sauce (use homemade evaporated milk) {found on page 158}

While wheat is definitely the "staff of life", there are a lot of other grains that can be useful in your long term food storage. White flour is good to include for making things like white sauces, pastries, etc. (and is critical if you don't have a wheat grinder yet). Oats can be used to give variety to your breakfasts and are a great comfort food.

This week's focus: BabyStep 5

Oats are available in many varieties such as quick rolled oats, regular rolled oats, steel cut oats, and oat groats. Quick oats cook faster but regular oats and steel cut oats retain flavor and nutrition better. Oat groats are the grain that the other varieties are made from, but you must roll, flake, or grind them yourself to make them into a usable oatmeal. We recommend storing one of the varieties besides quick oats as you would want the additional nutrition in a long term emergency situation. If you don't cook with or eat oats very often, try adding them into meals such as meat loaf, casseroles, and stews. They can be a great filler item to reduce how much meat you use.

TO PURCHASE:

✓ Purchase 25 lbs of white flour

✓ Purchase 50 lbs of regular rolled oats or other oat options

✓ Purchase 1 lb of baking soda

✓ Purchase some extra toothbrushes and some spare tubes of toothpaste

✓ Purchase something from your 3 month supply list, remember to update your list
  • Stock up on sale items, buy some things in bulk, or pick up a few extras items

TO DO:

✓ Read <u>All About Oats</u> {found on page 93}

RECIPES TO TRY:

❖ White Sauce Mac 'N' Cheese (uses powdered milk) {found on page 167}
❖ Grandma Lori's Sugar Cookies (uses white flour) {found on page 153}
❖ Granola Bars (uses oats) {found on page 153}
❖ Baked Oatmeal (uses oats and other food storage items) {found on page 141}

We are buying more wheat in this checklist and learning about the basics of bread-making. It's really not as hard as you think! You may even discover that you choose to make your own bread from now on versus using store-bought bread.

This week's focus: BabyStep 5

Food storage calculators include a lot of wheat in them because you can bake bread using wheat and only a few other basic ingredients. Bread will become the staple of your diet in a long term emergency situation where you are living exclusively off of your food storage. Bread-making and cooking with yeast can be very intimidating, but we encourage you to give it a try. The bread recipe listed below turns out great every time.

TO PURCHASE:

✓ Purchase 50 lbs of wheat

✓ Purchase 1 can of Vital Wheat Gluten (used in our favorite bread recipe)

✓ Purchase 1 lb of yeast

✓ Purchase some paper plates and paper towels to help reduce water consumption in an emergency. You may wish to purchase kleenex and/or baby wipes too.

✓ Purchase something from your 3 month supply list, remember to update your list
  • Stock up on sale items, buy some things in bulk, or pick up a few extras items

TO DO:

✓ Review articles that cover wheat {found on pages 92 and 102}

✓ Read <u>All About Yeast And Gluten</u> {found on page 122}

✓ Inventory and replenish your Non-Food items this week

✓ Learn about Bosch Mixers, WonderMix Mixers, and Kitchen-Aids as options for your bread-making appliance

RECIPES TO TRY:

❖ Best Whole Wheat Bread Recipe (our favorite recipe by far) {found on page 143}

This checklist is all about sugar! This may seem like a lot of sugar to store, but remember that in an emergency situation you will be making all of your foods from scratch and will be limited in what kind of sweeteners and flavorings you can use.

This week's focus: BabyStep 7

White granulated sugar doesn't spoil so it is a perfect food storage item. If it gets damp it will likely cake up or get lumpy. If it does, it can simply be pulverized again until it regains its granulated texture. Since sugar has such a long shelf life, you don't have to worry about rotating it if you don't care to use a lot of refined sugars in your everyday cooking. Simply store the recommended amount and know that you are covered if you need to use it eventually. You can also replace some of the sugar recommendation with honey or other sweeteners if you prefer them.

TO PURCHASE:

✓ Purchase 40 lbs of white sugar

✓ Purchase 1 lb of molasses (or any other alternate sweetener)

✓ Purchase one extra of the cleaners you use most often (all-purpose, Windex, etc.)

✓ Purchase something from your 3 month supply list, remember to update your list
  • Stock up on sale items, buy some things in bulk, or pick up a few extras items

TO DO:

✓ Review <u>All About Baking Ingredients: Sugars Section</u> {found on page 114}

✓ Read <u>All About Honey</u> if substituting some sugar with honey {found on page 117}

✓ Learn how to make your own homemade cleaners using basic supplies you already have on hand

RECIPES TO TRY:

❖ Cookie Clay Dough {found on page 148}
❖ Chocolate Cake {found on page 147}
❖ Homemade Brown Sugar (made with molasses) {found on page 145}

We are back to the grains category again but this time we are buying one that you might not normally think of for food storage ... PASTA. Pasta is cheap, easy, versatile, and best of all delicious!

This week's focus: BabyStep 5

Pasta is a great food storage item because a lot of pasta meals can be made completely with shelf stable ingredients. Pasta can be a really convenient grain to have on hand because it takes very little preparation compared to baked goods like bread, tortillas, etc. Remember if your storage is being used in time of natural disaster, pasta can use up a lot of water so plan to store extra water accordingly. If you are more interested in making your own whole wheat pasta you can store extra ingredients for that and less of the commercially-bought pastas.

TO PURCHASE:

✓ Purchase 50 lbs of pasta

✓ Purchase 8 lbs of salt

✓ Purchase a few extra bottles of shampoo and conditioner

✓ Purchase something from your 3 month supply list, remember to update your list
  • Stock up on sale items, buy some things in bulk, or pick up a few extras items

TO DO:

✓ Read <u>BabyStep 5 Introduction</u> {found on page 91}

✓ Research pasta makers if you decide you want to make homemade pastas

RECIPES TO TRY:

❖ Beach Street Lemon Chicken Linguine (uses pasta) {found on page 142}
❖ Meatballs Tetrazzini (uses pasta and freeze-dried ground beef) {found on page 159}
❖ Homemade Pasta (give it a try and decide if it works for you) {found on page 156}

This checklist is going to cover two food groups that aren't on traditional food storage calculators but can really add a lot of variety and/or nutrients to your food storage. We'll be learning more about freeze-dried cheese as well as adding fruits and vegetables to your storage.

This week's focus: BabySteps 7 & 8

Freeze-dried cheese is a food people don't often think of storing. However, we always say that if we could just eat pizza in an emergency, life would be ok. This seems silly but there is some truth to it. If you can make foods that your family is used to, they will handle a disaster situation much better. Freeze-dried cheese can be tricky to use so we recommend practicing with it a few times if you are planning to keep it in your storage.

Fruits and vegetables can be some of the most fun food storage items when you really get into planting a garden, canning, and dehydrating your own foods. If that thought overwhelms you, never fear ... we are starting simple! You'll notice that in the summertime lots of produce is available at great prices from farmer's markets and little neighborhood fruit stands. It's a great idea to stock up whenever fruit is on sale and freeze it in individual serving baggies. If that seems like too much work, you can just buy a few bags of frozen produce in order to always have some on hand.

TO PURCHASE:

✓ Purchase 1-2 pantry-sized cans of freeze-dried cheese to start experimenting with

✓ Purchase 3-4 bags of frozen fruit (or buy some fresh fruit and freeze it)

✓ Purchase something from your 3 month supply list, remember to update your list
   • Stock up on sale items, buy some things in bulk, or pick up a few extras items

TO DO:

✓ Read <u>All About Freeze-Dried Cheese</u> {found on page 120}

✓ Read <u>BabyStep 8 Introduction</u> {found on page 125}. Educate yourself on how to incorporate fruits and vegetables into your food storage.

RECIPES TO TRY:

❖ Cheesy Ritzy Potatoes (works well with freeze-dried cheese) {found on page 146}
❖ Whole Wheat Pizza Dough (try it with freeze-dried cheese) {found on page 168}
❖ Homemade Smoothies (use some of your frozen fruit) {found on page 157}

For this checklist we are going to work on some housekeeping items to make sure you are on track with your food storage goals. By now you should have your Emergency Preparedness Plan completed including your disaster kit, car kit, and 72 hour food kits. You should have some shelves set up and a water supply. Your three month supply should be growing. You have bought some basic long term food supply items, along with some extras. Now is also a good time to start thinking about how you will cook your foods if you don't have access to electricity in an emergency.

This week's focus: Maintenance & Education

Today's lesson is a reminder for you that food storage is going to be a constant part of your life. Disaster kits need to be updated as children grow. 72 hour kit food needs to be swapped out regularly. Water containers needs to be emptied and refilled once a year. We always need to be learning more and refining our plans. It's also a great idea to practice your powerless cooking now to really get the hang of it ... before you are in an emergency situation.

TO PURCHASE:

✓ Purchase a new shelf for more of your long term food storage

✓ Purchase or make a powerless cooking stove or appliance

✓ Purchase the grain mill or another kitchen appliance that you have been saving up for if you haven't already

✓ Purchase something from your 3 month supply list, remember to update your list
  • Stock up on sale items, buy some things in bulk, or pick up a few extras items

TO DO:

✓ Go through your Emergency Preparedness Plan with your family. Swap out outgrown or seasonal clothes and replace expired food/water. {found on pages 38-47}

✓ Educate yourself on more Emergency Prep topics by reading the following:
  • Last Minute Ways To Prepare {found on page 48}
  • Emergency Heat Sources {found on page 50}
  • Ways to Keep Cool with No Power {found on page 51}
  • Emergency Sanitation Kits {found on page 53}
  • Planning Your Future {found on page 55}
  • Powerless Cooking Stoves/Ovens {found on page 56}
  • Emergency Cooking Fuels {found on page 58}

We're adding to our legumes in this checklist, but we are going to teach you some fun new ways to use them! Make sure to add some white beans such as lima beans to your storage and you can make a great bean flour that can be used for lots of things.

This week's focus: BabyStep 6

We already talked about how mashed beans can replace the oil or butter in a lot of recipes to reduce the fat/calories and increase the fiber and protein. Another surprising thing you can do with beans is to grind white beans into a flour which can be used to make a healthy, delicious white sauce or any condensed cream soup by just adding a few simple ingredients. Any recipe that calls for white sauce (butter, flour, liquid) or cream of chicken/mushroom/celery soup can easily be made healthier and lower fat by replacing it with bean flour.

TO PURCHASE:

✓ Purchase 25 lbs of dried beans (make sure to include some white beans to grind)

✓ Purchase 2 qts of mayonnaise

✓ Purchase a few extra sticks of deodorant for each family member

✓ Purchase something from your 3 month supply list, remember to update your list
  • Stock up on sale items, buy some things in bulk, or pick up a few extras items

TO DO:

✓ Read <u>All About Dried Beans</u> {found on page 104}

✓ Practice grinding beans and using them as a replacement for white or creamy sauces in your own recipes

RECIPES TO TRY:

❖ White Sauce Mac 'N' Cheese (legume substitutions version) {found on page 167}
❖ Cream of Chicken Soup (uses bean flour) {found on page 149}
❖ Creamy Potato Soup (uses bean flour) {found on page 150}
❖ Enchilada Pie (full of food storage substitutions) {found on page 151}

We're going to do something a little non-traditional in this checklist. Traditional food storage calculators do not have you store powdered eggs. However, we have found that there are a LOT of great foods we could make if we simply added that one ingredient to our food storage. We have added some powdered eggs into our plan so that you can have more variety in your cooking.

This week's focus: BabyStep 7

Beyond the benefits of storing powdered eggs for an emergency, there are some great benefits to using them in your everyday cooking. First, powdered eggs are not RAW so if you love to eat cookie dough but are worried about salmonella, you will LOVE using powdered eggs. Second, powdered eggs are great to have on hand for those days you go to cook dinner and realize you are out of eggs and you need them for a recipe. We love using food storage for even those small "emergencies". Finally, powdered eggs can be used to make a lot of your own pre-made mixes instead of having to add regular eggs in later.

TO PURCHASE:

✓ Purchase 2 lbs of whole powdered eggs (or other powdered egg varieties)

✓ Purchase 1 lb of flavored gelatin

✓ Purchase a few extra bottles of dish soap

✓ Purchase some extra containers of dish detergent

✓ Purchase something from your 3 month supply list, remember to update your list
  • Stock up on sale items, buy some things in bulk, or pick up a few extras items

TO DO:

✓ Read All About Powdered Eggs {found on page 116}

RECIPES TO TRY:

❖ Blender Wheat Pancakes (uses powdered eggs) {found on page 144}
❖ Homemade Egg McMuffins (uses powdered egg whites) {found on page 154}
❖ Buttermilk Cornbread (uses powdered eggs) {found on page 145}
❖ Homemade Mayonnaise (uses powdered eggs) {found on page 155}
❖ Patriotic Jello (uses gelatin) {found on page 160}

For this checklist we are purchasing some more wheat and giving you new ideas on how to use it. We are also introducing one of our favorite preparedness-related hobbies ... gardening! Learning how to grow a few foods, even just in the kitchen, can be a big help in times of emergency when it becomes a necessity.

This week's focus: BabySteps 5 & 8

Gardening can be overwhelming. The best way to start gardening is to try growing a few simple herbs on your window sill that you can start using in your cooking. This will give you the confidence you need to move on to new things. Most vegetables can be grown in large pots either on your deck/patio or even inside if you have the space in your kitchen. Some easy ones to try are lettuce and tomatoes. Once you are able to do that, you may want to consider building some garden boxes in your yard and expanding your gardening horizons to include enough veggies to eat all summer, as well as enough to can, freeze, and dehydrate for your long term food storage.

TO PURCHASE:

✓ Purchase 50 lbs of wheat

✓ Purchase some gardening seeds for items you can grow in your kitchen or patio

✓ Purchase something from your 3 month supply list, remember to update your list
   • Stock up on sale items, buy some things in bulk, or pick up a few extras items

TO DO:

✓ Review articles that cover wheat {found on pages 92 and 102}

✓ Read <u>All About Square Foot Gardening</u> {found on page 129}

✓ Read <u>How To Build A Vinyl Square Foot Garden Box</u> {found on page 131} if you plan on building your own garden boxes.

✓ Start some herbs or smaller vegetables growing in your kitchen

RECIPES TO TRY:

❖ Whole Wheat Tortillas (100% wheat or half white/half wheat) {found on page 169}
❖ Enchilada Pie (uses the tortillas you made) {found on page 151}

We're moving on to storing two new grains in this checklist. Rice is a staple food for families in many societies as it is inexpensive, has a long storage life, and is very versatile. Barley is also a great grain with a long shelf life and many uses.

This week's focus: BabyStep 5

White rice has a shelf life typically of up to 30 years if stored properly. This makes it an ideal food storage food. Brown rice has a much shorter shelf life (6 months to a year). If your family prefers brown rice, we suggest storing only as much brown rice as your family would normally eat in 6 months. The rest of the recommended amount should be stored in white rice. Barley can be used in many soups and stews and it can be ground into a flour and added to breads or other baked goods.

TO PURCHASE:

✓ Purchase 40 lbs of rice

✓ Purchase 10 lbs of barley

✓ Purchase 1/2 gallon of vinegar

✓ Purchase some extras of the body wash or soap that your family uses

✓ Purchase something from your 3 month supply list, remember to update your list
  • Stock up on sale items, buy some things in bulk, or pick up a few extras items

TO DO:

✓ Read <u>All About Rice</u> {found on page 94}

✓ Read <u>All About Barley</u> {found on page 96}

✓ Research rice cookers and electric pressure cookers and save up for one if desired

✓ Try using vinegar in some of your cleaning chores

RECIPES TO TRY:

❖ Chow Mein Casserole (uses rice, white or brown) {found on page 147}
❖ Homemade Rice-A-Roni {found on page 157}
❖ Rice Pudding {found on page 164}
❖ Chicken Barley Chili {found on page 146}
❖ Wonderflour (white flour substitute that uses rice and barley) {found on page 169}

This checklist is going to cover buying some of the food storage "powders" as well as teach you about canning. If you are planning to incorporate fruits and vegetables into your year supply, canning is a great way to do it.

This week's focus: BabySteps 7 & 8

If there were an emergency situation where you had to eat out of your food storage, your diet would be boring if you stuck with the basic food storage recommendations. Adding in powders such as sour cream and butter can help add variety to your meals.

Storing fruits and vegetables is another way to decrease diet fatigue and add nutrition in an emergency. We've already discussed storing some frozen produce, but having canned items is also a great addition. You can purchase store-bought cans of most produce items but they retain less nutrients, cost more, and have a lot more preservatives added in. Home canning is a great way to get a lot of food stockpiled inexpensively, all at once, and it's actually pretty fun to do it!

TO PURCHASE:

✓ Purchase 1-2 pantry-sized cans of dairy powders to try

✓ Purchase 3 lbs of brown sugar

✓ Purchase some canning supplies such as a canner, tongs, jars, lids, etc.

✓ Purchase something from your 3 month supply list, remember to update your list
   • Stock up on sale items, buy some things in bulk, or pick up a few extras items

TO DO:

✓ Read <u>All About Powdered Butter</u> {found on page 118}

✓ Read <u>All About Powdered Sour Cream</u> {found on page 119}

✓ Read <u>All About Canning</u> {found on page 128}

✓ Try a canning project. A good place to start is applesauce, peaches, or tomatoes.

RECIPES TO TRY:

❖ Sugar Bars (uses brown sugar) {found on page 165}
❖ Poppyseed Chicken (uses powdered sour cream and butter) {found on page 162}

For this checklist we are going to give you some great new non-wheat recipes to keep your family from getting tired of wheat if you are eating purely out of food storage. Cornmeal is a fantastic food to store but a lot of people don't know how to use it. We're going to remedy that in this checklist.

This week's focus: BabyStep 5

Cornmeal is ground similarly to flour. Store-bought cornmeal has the husk and germ of the kernel almost completely removed and therefore has a very long shelf life. If you want a healthier version, you can grind your own corn kernels to make cornmeal. It's best to grind it right before use to avoid losing nutrients and keep it from going rancid. Cornmeal or corn kernels are a welcome addition to food storage to help avoid diet fatigue. We've had fun coming up with lots of different uses for cornmeal and have included some of the recipes for you to try in the recipe appendix.

TO PURCHASE:

✓ Purchase 25 lbs of cornmeal (or store corn kernels if you have a wheat grinder)

✓ Purchase 1 lb of baking powder

✓ Purchase a few extra razors and bottles of shaving cream for each family member

✓ Purchase something from your 3 month supply list, remember to update your list
  • Stock up on sale items, buy some things in bulk, or pick up a few extras items

TO DO:

✓ Read All About Cornmeal/Popcorn {found on page 95}

RECIPES TO TRY:

❖ Corncakes {found on page 149}
❖ Corn Dog Muffins {found on page 148}
❖ Buttermilk Cornbread {found on page 145}

We will be collecting the last of our powdered milk for this checklist and we'll also be talking about dehydrated and freeze-dried fruits and vegetables. Adding fruits and vegetables to your storage is a great way to add variety and nutrition to your diet .

This week's focus: BabyStep 7

Let's talk about the benefits of dehydrated or freeze-dried foods. Not only are they great for an emergency, but they are convenient in everyday cooking. Using pre-cut veggies cuts way back on meal prep time. Freeze-dried fruits can help you make a dessert, or healthy shake in a pinch. We recommend starting out by being a few #10 cans to test them out. You can continue to buy cans or eventually invest in a home dehydrator or freeze-drying machine if the do-it-your-self approach appeals to you.

TO PURCHASE:

✓ Purchase 8 lbs of non-instant dry milk (double this amount if storing instant dry milk)

✓ Purchase 3 lbs of corn syrup and 3 lbs of jam, any flavor

✓ Purchase a few #10 cans of dehydrated or freeze-dried fruits and vegetables

✓ Purchase something from your 3 month supply list, remember to update your list
   • Stock up on sale items, buy some things in bulk, or pick up a few extras items

TO DO:

✓ Read <u>All About Food Dehydration</u> {found on page 126}

✓ Read <u>All About Freeze-Drying</u> {found on page 127}

✓ Research more about food dehydrators and home freeze-drying machines

✓ Review <u>All About Powdered Milk</u> {found on page 115}

✓ Refer to <u>Food Storage Equivalents Chart</u> {found on page 140}

RECIPES TO TRY:

❖ Blackberry Pie (uses freeze-dried berries) {found on page 144}
❖ Tortellini Chicken Soup (uses freeze-dried/dehydrated veggies) {found on page 166}
❖ Buttermilk Cornbread (uses homemade buttermilk) {found on page 145}
❖ Best Rice Krispie Squares (uses corn syrup) {found on page 143}
❖ Worms and Dirt Pudding Treat (uses powdered milk) {found on page 169}

We are going to purchase some more legumes for this checklist. We are stocking up on lentils and dry soup mix. Dry soup mixes are things like onion soup, chicken or beef bouillon, 12 bean soup mix, etc. Basically any kind of seasoning that would flavor a delicious soup/stew that uses your beans.

This week's focus: BabyStep 7

What is a lentil and how do you use it? A lentil is the round flat seed of a lentil plant. Lentils are often cooked like peas, added to soups and stews, or even eaten plain. You can also grind them into meal to use as an additive. Or you can make a nice leafy sprout to add to salads or as filler for meats and casseroles. Lentil sprouts taste similar to fresh peas. Lentils are VERY healthy as they are high in fiber, can help reduce cholesterol, and give you more energy. What better food could you ask for in an emergency situation? Don't be afraid to give them a try.

TO PURCHASE:

✓ Purchase 5 lbs of lentils

✓ Purchase 2 lbs of dry soup mix (or bouillons to flavor soups)

✓ Purchase 2 gallons of vegetable oil

✓ Purchase a few extra packages of diapers (or any other non-food item)

✓ Purchase something from your 3 month supply list, remember to update your list
  • Stock up on sale items, buy some things in bulk, or pick up a few extras items

TO DO:

✓ Read <u>All About Other Legumes</u> {found on page 106}

✓ Read <u>All About Sprouting</u> and give sprouting a try {found on page 107}

✓ Read <u>15 Ways To Use Sprouts</u> {found on page 108}

RECIPES TO TRY:

❖ Greek Lentil Soup {found on page 154}
❖ Curried Lentils and Rice {found on page 150}
❖ Ezekiel Bread (uses lentils and other grains and legumes) {found on page 152}

This week we are covering two more areas that are not on traditional food storage calculators. We will learn about adding meats into your food storage plan and also purchasing some spices. It would not be fun to end up in an emergency situation and be stuck cooking bland meals without any of your normal flavorings.

This week's focus: BabySteps 6 & 9

Most long term food storage plans account for our protein needs through legumes. We recommend storing legumes and getting used to using them. It's also nice to have some meats in your storage. You can store canned (or home-canned) meats, frozen meats, dehydrated meats, or freeze-dried meats. If you want long shelf life then freeze-dried is best, however it is great to have other options as well.

There are many reasons that you should store extra spices as part of your food storage plan. First off, don't you hate it when you run out of a spice JUST as you are cooking dinner? Wouldn't it be great to know you have an extra bottle in the basement? Also, spices quite often go on sale or have coupons available for brand name products. If you can stock up at lower prices you save a lot of money.

TO PURCHASE:

✓ Purchase 1-2 pantry-sized cans of freeze-dried meat to test out

✓ Purchase a few extra bottles of spare spices

✓ Purchase something from your 3 month supply list, remember to update your list
  • Stock up on sale items, buy some things in bulk, or pick up a few extras items

TO DO:

✓ Read All About Meats {found on page 109}

✓ Read Using Freeze-Dried Meats {found on page 111}

✓ Read All About Spices And Condiments {found on page 133}

✓ Document which spices you use regularly and make a plan for storing extras

RECIPES TO TRY:

❖ Tortellini Chicken Soup (uses freeze-dried chicken) {found on page 166}
❖ Pizza Casserole (uses freeze-dried sausage crumbles) {found on page 162}
❖ Mexican Casserole (uses freeze-dried ground beef) {found on page 161}

This is our final checklist to work on legumes. Can you believe we are almost done? The final legume we'll be storing is split peas. If you don't care for split peas you are always welcome to replace them with a different legume. However, once you try a few recipes using them you may decide you like them.

This week's focus: BabyStep 6

Split peas are the dried, peeled, and split seeds of Pisum sativum (peas). They come in yellow and green varieties. They have been mechanically split so that they will cook faster, this can be helpful when needing to conserve fuel in a long term emergency situation. They are a great source of protein and have a long shelf life so they are a good way to get some variety in your legume storage. Split peas are most often used in soups and stews to add texture and nutrition.

TO PURCHASE:

✓ Purchase 5 lbs of split peas

✓ Purchase 4 lbs of peanut butter

✓ Purchase a 6 month supply of toilet paper

✓ Purchase something from your 3 month supply list, remember to update your list
  • Stock up on sale items, buy some things in bulk, or pick up a few extras items

TO DO:

✓ Read <u>All About Other Legumes</u> {found on page 106}

RECIPES TO TRY:

❖ Pea Soup {found on page 161}
❖ 12 Bean Soup (includes split peas) {found on page 141}
❖ Peanut Butter Bread {found on page 161}
❖ Best Rice Krispie Squares (uses peanut butter) {found on page 143}
❖ No-Bake Peanut Butter Energy Bites {found on page 160}

For this checklist we will be buying the last of our wheat, another sugar item, and also covering an aspect of comfort foods that we haven't talked about yet - condiments. This will also be the last time we remind you to continue to build and replenish your Three Month Supply. Hopefully by now it is a habit ingrained in you and you will naturally do it in your normal grocery shopping.

This week's focus: BabySteps 5 & 9

Condiments are similar to spices in that there are a lot of reasons why it makes a lot of sense to store extras. First of all, don't you hate when you make a delicious steak dinner, just to find out you are out of A1 sauce? It is great to know that you always have at least one spare bottle on hand of all condiments. Also, things like ketchup and mustard come on sale and/or have coupons every now and then. Wouldn't you like to buy your mustard during a sale, instead of paying full price when you are desperate and have none left? Finally, in an emergency situation, condiments can add a lot of flavor and "comfort" to the foods that you will be living off of.

TO PURCHASE:

✓ Purchase 50 lbs of wheat

✓ Purchase 6 lbs of fruit flavored drink (helps stored water taste better)

✓ Purchase at least one spare of each of your condiments

✓ Purchase something from your 3 month supply list, remember to update your list
  • Stock up on sale items, buy some things in bulk, or pick up a few extras items

TO DO:

✓ Review articles that cover wheat {found on pages 92 and 102}

✓ Practice substituting fresh ground wheat flour for white flour in your regular baking

✓ Review All About Spices And Condiments {found on page 133}

RECIPES TO TRY:

❖ Whole Wheat Pumpkin Cake {found on page 168}

By the end of this checklist we will have completed all of the BabySteps. In this checklist we are going to be tying up loose ends by storing medicines and first aid items as well as taking care of any needs for our pets. We will be taking care of some housekeeping items such as water rotation and disaster kit evaluation. We will also give you some ideas on where to go from here as you continue on your food storage journey.

This week's focus: BabyStep 10 & Maintenance

During a natural disaster medical attention is often hard to come by. It is always a good idea to have basic first aid supplies on hand, as well as a working knowledge of how to use them. This can come in handy in everyday emergency situations as well. Medicines have limited shelf life but there are some great alternatives that are very useful in your food storage such as essential oils and other natural remedies.

Pets are always an important part of any family's emergency preparedness plans. We wanted to make sure human needs were addressed first but didn't want you to finish your preparedness program without accounting for your pets as well. Determine how much food would be necessary for their year supply and add that in to your storage.

TO PURCHASE:

✓ Purchase a basic first aid kit and any additional useful medical supplies

✓ Purchase extra medicines or essential oils to help with minor ailments

✓ Purchase food and supplies necessary for your pets as desired

TO DO:

✓ Read Basic CPR and First Aid Tips {found on page 135}

✓ Re-evaluate your Emergency Preparedness Plan {found on pages 38-47} and remind young children of the family plan

✓ Go through your Disaster Kit and swap out children's outgrown or seasonal clothing

✓ Eat the contents from your 72 Hour Kits and replace them with unexpired foods

✓ Empty your water containers and refill with fresh water

✓ Remember to keep on working on your food storage, as it's a continual process

PART TWO

FOOD STORAGE ENCYCLOPEDIA

The Food Storage Encyclopedia section of this book includes everything you need to know about building a Food Storage. Each of the articles referenced in the checklists can be found in these pages. Feel free to read through the entire book or reference individual articles as indicated while you work through each list.

Now before we get started, let's answer the obvious: **WHY FOOD STORAGE?**

NATURAL DISASTERS:

One of the most common reasons people decide to build a food storage and have an emergency preparedness plan is in case of a natural disaster. Between storms, earthquakes, terrorist attacks, and a myriad of scenarios that could occur, it is wise to be prepared for the unknown.

ECONOMIC CRISIS:

Whether it be a national economic crisis, or a personal crisis through job loss, being prepared for uncertain financial situations is wise and prudent. You never know what could happen and it's such a blessing to have food stored and a plan in place for a time when you might have to live off of what you have stored.

HEALTH BENEFITS

Some typical foods recommended in food storage programs include whole grains and legumes. When cooking with these items and making meals from scratch you are able to avoid a lot of preservatives and additives. Not only does storing food help prepare you for uncertainty, using it can open up a lot of healthy options that are low-calorie, low-fat, high in protein, and high in fiber.

EVERYDAY EMERGENCIES

While you would never think of starting to build your food storage to prepare for "everyday emergencies", it sure is a nice side benefit once you have some spare food accumulated. When you are missing an ingredient, you don't have to run to the store if you have it in your food storage. Sometimes you are called at the last minute to bring meals, snacks, or treats to people or events. It's convenient and saves you extra money you might spend on last minute trips to the store.

RELIGIOUS REASONS

If you start researching "Food Storage", you probably know that it is a very common practice among members of the Church of Jesus Christ of Latter Day Saints (and some other religions) to have a food storage. Leaders of the many faiths have long counseled members to be prepare for uncertainties.

EMERGENCY PREPAREDNESS:

INTRODUCTION:

★ Use our Emergency Preparedness Plan as a guide to develop your own family plan

★ Take into consideration family members with special needs and/or pets

★ Customize your plan to fit the preferences of you and your family

★ Take care of the basics first, don't get overwhelmed with more advanced topics

★ In addition to a preparedness plan, backup your computers and other digital media

★ Make sure you have proper insurance, wills, and other legal documents in place

★ Start thinking about alternate fuel/cooking sources, sanitation, etc.

★ Emergency Preparedness Plan sections:

- **Family Plan:** Includes a list of topics to discuss with your family, emergency protocol to follow, contact info, meeting locations and education. An emergency is no time to figure out what you should be doing. Make it a habit of reminding young children of your plans and protocols.

- **72 Hour Kit & Emergency Binder:** Includes a list of items for 72 hour kits. We've also included a list of important documents for you to gather to create your Emergency Binder in case you you have to "rebuild" your life. These items may be for you to use at home, or for you to take with you in case of an evacuation type scenario.

- **Evacuation List & Car Kit:** Includes measures to take when evacuating your home including a list of important things to grab and instructions to build a car kit. You never know when you may be stranded on the road, so make sure to keep your car prepared for emergencies.

INSIDE THIS SECTION:

Emergency Preparedness Plan
Last Minute Ways To Prepare
Emergency Heat Sources
Ways to Keep Cool Without Power
Emergency Sanitation Kits
Emergency Kits for Babies
Planning Your Future
Powerless Cooking Stoves/Ovens
Emergency Cooking Fuels

MY EMERGENCY PREPAREDNESS PLAN

FAMILY PLAN

Includes a list of topics to discuss with your family, emergency protocol to follow, contact info, meeting locations and education.

An emergency is no time to figure out what you should be doing. Make it a habit of reminding young children of your plans and protocols.

72 HOUR KIT & EMERGENCY BINDER

Includes a list of items to have on hand, for your disaster kit, along with options for you to get a 72-hour food kit assembled.

Also included is a list of important documents for you to gather in case you have to "rebuild" your life.

EVACUATION LIST AND CAR KIT

Includes measures to take when evacuating your home including a list of important things to grab should you need to evacuate.

You never know when you may be stranded on the road, so make sure to keep your car prepared for emergencies.

FAMILY PLAN

It's a good idea to be on the same page with your family as to what you would do in case of an emergency. Review these concepts every few months as we all can be forgetful.

DISCUSSION POINTS:

★ Meet with family members to discuss how to respond to the dangers of fire, severe weather, earthquakes, and other emergencies

★ Find safe spots in your home for each type of disaster

★ Discuss what to do about power outages

★ Draw a floor plan of your home and mark two escape routes from each room

★ Post emergency phone numbers near telephones

★ Teach children how and when to call 911

★ Instruct family members to turn on radio for information

★ Pick one out-of-state and one local contact person to call in case of a disaster.

★ Teach children phone numbers.

★ Pick two reunion locations one right outside of your home, and one away from your neighborhood in case you cannot return

★ Take a basic first aid and CPR class

★ Revise and review the plan with your family regularly

IN CASE OF EVACUATION
CONSIDER LEAVING A NOTE
ON YOUR DOOR FOR PEOPLE
WHO MAY COME TO YOUR
HOUSE LOOKING FOR YOU

TO FILL OUT:

OUT-OF-STATE CONTACT:

Name:

City:

Telephone:

LOCAL CONTACT:

Name:

Telephone:

NEAREST RELATIVE:

Name:

Telephone:

FAMILY WORK NUMBERS:

Mother:

Father:

EMERGENCY TELEPHONE NUMBERS:

Police Department:

Fire Department:

Hospital:

FAMILY PHYSICIANS:

Name:

Telephone:

Name:

Telephone:

REUNION LOCATIONS:

Right outside home:

Address:

Away from home:

Address:

Telephone:

Route to try first:

72 HOUR KITS

72 hour kits contain items you may need to deal with different situations in a disaster along with food and water to last you at least 72 hours. Food will be covered in the following pages.

ITEMS TO INCLUDE IN YOUR KIT:

- √ Water supply
- √ Food (see next page)
- √ First aid kit
- √ Prescription medications
- √ Extra pair of glasses
- √ Contact solution
- √ Credit cards and cash
- √ Change of clothes
- √ Sturdy shoes
- √ Battery powered radio
- √ Extra batteries
- √ Blankets or sleeping bags
- √ Rain poncho

- √ Body warmer
- √ Glow stick
- √ Tarp or a tent
- √ List of contact info
- √ Jumper cables for car
- √ Car shovel
- √ Ropes
- √ Swiss army knife
- √ N95 dust mask
- √ Work gloves
- √ Flashlights
- √ Wind/waterproof matches
- √ Candles and lighter

- √ Trash bags
- √ Personal hygiene products
- √ Baby supplies
- √ Games and books
- √ Pet supplies
- √ Sanitation supplies
- √ Tire repair kit and pump
- √ Maps of surrounding areas
- √ Sewing kit
- √ Blank CD for SOS
- √ Whistle
- √ Multipurpose tool
- √ PowerCap

PURCHASING ITEMS FOR YOUR KIT:

★ Start by gathering things from your home that you already have

★ Make gathering your supplies a fun family activity

★ Create a scavenger hunt or treasure hunt with small kids

★ Spread your purchases out over time, don't go into debt

★ Remind your family that preparedness products make great gifts

★ Purchase trial size toiletries, or save hotel toiletries, for your kit

SAVE ROOM IN YOUR KITS BY STORING THINGS YOU MAY NEED FOR COLDER WEATHER IN A SEPARATE BAG

CONSIDER PURCHASING EXTRA CLOTHES FOR YOUR KIT FROM THRIFT STORES

72 HOUR KITS: Food Options

The next few pages will tackle food for your 72 hour kit. You should tailor the food in your kits to your needs.

Regardless of what you pack for food, here are some universal considerations:

COOKING SUPPLIES:

✓ Plastic utensils
✓ Paper plates
✓ Cups
✓ Matches
✓ Can opener (if needed)
✓ Fire starter packets
✓ Cooking stove
✓ Fuel

ROTATION IDEAS:

★ Rotate according to shelf life
★ Rotate the same time of year
★ Use food on camping trips
★ Purchase foods you like so rotating won't be hard
★ Check your food often to make sure it's still good

IN CASE OF EVACUATION IF CIRCUMSTANCES PERMIT, GRAB AS MUCH FOOD FROM YOUR PANTRY AND KITCHEN AS POSSIBLE

DETAILED INSTRUCTIONS

If you want it all laid out for you including a step-by-step shopping list and contents list, follow our 72 hour kit milk jug instructions.

CREATE YOUR OWN

If you want to have more flexibility, you can customize your kit using our meal planner worksheet and choose foods from our sample menus.

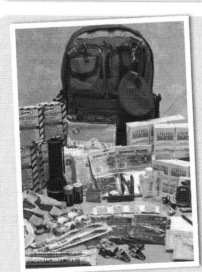

PURCHASE READY MADE

If you don't have the time (or energy) to build your own kits there are a lot of options available for purchase that may suit your needs.

72 HOUR KITS: Detailed Instructions For Food

These are instructions for assembling 72 hours worth of food. The shopping list and menu found on the next page contain the foods you will need to buy and a menu for eating them over 72 hours.

MILK JUG KIT INSTRUCTIONS:

STEP 1 – Make sure you have one clean milk jug and 3 2 liter bottle of water per person.

STEP 2 – Multiply the number of kits you want by the items listed in shopping list and purchase the food items.

STEP 3 – Purchase a small stove and fuel pellets from an emergency preparedness store. Only one stove is necessary per family, but they are quite inexpensive, so if you'd like to have one per kit that is fine too. It will make it much more convenient in a true emergency.

STEP 4 – Cut straight down the middle of a milk jug diagonal from the handle. Go about 1/3 of the way down. At the bottom of that cut, make a horizontal slice coming from each side but leave about 2 inches of the jug intact. This should make a little door that you can pull open and insert the items into the jug.

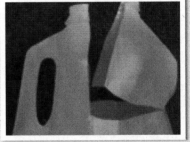

STEP 5 – Place the necessary items into each milk jug according to the contents list. Put the Tang and cocoa servings into small zip-lock bags (1/4 c. per serving). If you have extra food left over, stick it in as space permits. Tape the milk jug closed. Tape the contents list to the outside of the jug and record today's date and the family member who will use that kit.

*Please note this kit is very basic and may not be enough food to stay comfortable. However some people like its simplicity, detailed instructions, and the fact that in all fits into a milk jug.

72 HOUR KIT: Milk Jug Kit Shopping List and Menu

SHOPPING LIST:

	# per kit	# kits	Total to buy
Tang (1/4 cup each serving)	2 servings		
Instant oatmeal	2 packets		
Granola bars	2 servings		
Cocoa mix (1/4 cup each)	2 servings		
Single serving stew with "pop top lid"	1 can		
Gum	9 sticks		
Candies (that wont melt)	9 pieces		
Beans and Wieners with "pop top lid"	1 can		
Fruit roll-up	3		
Single serving Lipton noodles	2 pouches		
1 oz package raisins	1		
1 oz package beef jerky	2 packages		
Plastic spoons	3		
Matches	1 package		
Snack-size zip lock bags for Tang and cocoa	4 bags		
Clear packing tape to close	6 inches		
Wing stove	1 stove		
Fuel pellets	3 packages		
Misc extras			

⇒ This kit requires a 2-liter bottle of water to reconstitute the foods included
⇒ Mix 3/4 cup water with Tang and hot cocoa mix
⇒ Save and reuse the Beans and Wieners can to heat other foods if needed
⇒ 3 (2-liter) bottles of water are suggested for each person

MENU:

DAY 1 - BREAKFAST:
Tang and Oatmeal

DAY 1 - LUNCH:
Beans and Wieners
Fruit Roll-Up

DAY 1 - DINNER:
Granola bar
Beef jerky
Hot cocoa mix

DAY 1 - SNACK:
3 pieces of gum
3 pieces of candy

DAY 2 - BREAKFAST:
Hot cocoa and Granola bar

DAY 2 - LUNCH:
Lipton soup
Raisins

DAY 2 - DINNER:
Stew
Fruit roll-up

DAY 2 - SNACK:
3 pieces of gum
3 pieces of candy

DAY 3 - BREAKFAST:
Tang and Oatmeal

DAY 3 - LUNCH:
Lipton soup

DAY 3 - DINNER:
Beef Jerky
Fruit roll-up
Hot cocoa mix

DAY 3 - SNACK:
3 pieces of gum
3 pieces of candy

NAME:_____
DATE PACKED:_____
(use within 1 year)

72 HOUR KITS: Create Your Own Options

Here are some ideas based on various diets and preferences that can be used to fill out the meal planner worksheet found on the next page. Don't be afraid to tailor your 72 hour kit of food to your own liking. Remember vacuum sealing foods can help extend their shelf life.

SAMPLE MENUS:

REGULAR FOOD OPTIONS:
- Granola bars
- Chocolate candy/chips
- Dried/dehydrated fruits
- Tuna pouches
- Wheat crackers for the tuna
- Raw almonds
- Hot cocoa
- Fruit drink mix
- Ramen noodles/cup of noodles
- Jerky
- Pouches of soup mixes
- Canned raviolis or like foods
- Peanut butter
- Small jar of jelly
- Small container honey
- Banana chips
- Protein powder
- Gatorade

MINIMAL ROTATION OPTIONS:
- Emergency food bars
- MRE meals: spaghetti, chili mac, breakfast skillet, chicken and rice, beef stroganoff
- MRE Meals can last up to 25 years, but remember to store water and cooking fuel

"HEALTHIER" OPTIONS:
- Plain instant oatmeal
- Apple chips (vacuum seal them)
- Bush's baked beans pop top
- Pouches of "squeeze" fruit
- Chunk light tuna in water
- 2-3 foil packets of condiments
- Shelton's Chili
- Granola bars
- Resealable bags of dried fruit
- Lunchbox size packs of crackers
- Laughing Cow cheese wedges
- Himalayan pink salt
- Crystal Light Pure
- Packet of Emergen-C

GLUTEN FREE OPTIONS:
- Larabars
- Lundberg Rice Cakes
- GF Granola (like Bakery on Main)
- Beef Jerky
- Can of Chicken or Tuna
- Mary's Gone Crackers
- Dinty Moore Beef Stew
- Hormel Chili
- Applesauce
- Canned Fruit
- Fruit Leather
- Fruit Roll-up or Fruit Snacks
- Raisins
- Boxes of Pacific Almond Milk
- Peanut or other Nut Butter
- Honey

VEGAN OPTIONS:
- Cliff bars
- Lara bars
- Nut bars
- Vitamin B12 tablet
- Bar of vegan dark chocolate
- Peanut butter
- Nuts packaged in vacuum bags
- Seeds packaged in vacuum bags
- Prepackaged precooked meals (the Indian dishes that can be found in mylar bags work well)

NO COOK OPTIONS:
- Cereal bars
- Crackers
- Peanut butter
- Pudding cups
- Fruit cups
- Fruit roll-ups
- Cans of vegetables
- Pork and beans (can eat cold)
- Granola bars
- Chocolate candy/chips
- Dried fruits/dehydrated fruits
- Almonds

KID-FRIENDLY FOODS:
- Tuna pouch
- Chicken pouch
- Canned peas, carrots
- Crackers
- Craisins, & other dried fruit
- Fruit snacks or other candy treat
- Cheerios in sealed bag
- Canned fruit
- Single serving milk packets
- Granola bars
- Hormel complete meals – chicken & rice or turkey & mashed potatoes
- Include games, books, crayons etc

CONSIDERATIONS FOR BABIES:
- Instant formula
- Plenty of diapers or cloth diapers
- A travel package of wipes
- Pacifiers
- 3 cotton/flannel wraps
- Baby food
- Washcloths
- Small comfort toys
- Lots of spare clothes
- Ziplock bags
- Bulb nose syringe and saline
- Infant tylenol/motrin
- Desitin or other diaper rash cream and travel-sized baby powder

CAT KIT (alter for other pets):
- 1 gallon of water
- 1 plastic gallon jug with dry food
- 1 12 pack box of wet food packets
- 1 small bag of treats
- Small litterbox and scoop
- Plastic gallon jug with kitty litter
- Small plastic trash bags
- Towel
- Mini pet first aid kit
- Vaccination/vet records
- Color photo of cat
- Extra collar w/contact info
- Leash and harness

MEAL PLANNER WORKSHEET

DAY 1:

BREAKFAST:

_____
_____
_____
_____

SNACK:

_____
_____
_____

LUNCH:

_____
_____
_____
_____

SNACK:

_____
_____
_____

DINNER:

_____
_____
_____
_____

DAY 2:

BREAKFAST:

_____
_____
_____
_____

SNACK:

_____
_____
_____

LUNCH:

_____
_____
_____
_____

SNACK:

_____
_____
_____

DINNER:

_____
_____
_____
_____

DAY 3:

BREAKFAST:

_____
_____
_____
_____

SNACK:

_____
_____
_____

LUNCH:

_____
_____
_____
_____

SNACK:

_____
_____
_____

DINNER:

_____
_____
_____
_____

EXTRA NOTES AND CONSIDERATIONS:

_____
_____
_____
_____

EMERGENCY BINDER

An emergency binder is a compilation of important documents. Store your binder in a fireproof/waterproof locked box that is small enough to be transported with you in an evacuation situation.

ITEMS TO INCLUDE IN YOUR EMERGENCY BINDER:

VITAL DOCUMENTS

√ Birth certificates

√ Passports

√ Immunization records

√ CASH – keep small bills

√ Copy of your will

√ Medical information

√ Military and church papers

√ Diplomas and transcripts

√ Marriage certificates

√ Adoption papers

√ Current pictures of family

√ Pet records

√ Proof of citizenship

INSURANCE INFORMATION

√ Homeowners insurance policy

√ Auto insurance policy

√ Life insurance policy

√ Medical insurance policy

√ Pictures and lists of all your personal belongings for insurance

√ Contact information for insurance agents

SOME PEOPLE TAKE VIDEOS OF EACH ROOM OF THEIR HOUSE AS A WAY OF DOCUMENTING THEIR BELONGINGS FOR INSURANCE

FINANCIAL INFORMATION

√ Copies of your credit cards front and back

√ Bank statements

√ Retirement statements

√ Social security statements

√ Internet passwords (banking, personal, work etc.)

√ Utility statements

√ Work/tax documents that would be difficult to replace

√ Deeds to properties

√ Titles to cars, boats, etc.

√ Warranty information

PREPARE MY LIFE PLANNER:

The Prepare My Life Planner is an organized emergency preparedness plan. Not only is it designed to store and organize all your important documents, it **ALSO contains a step-by-step plan to help prepare your home and family for an emergency**.

★ **Sections:** Prepare My Family, Prepare My Home, Gather Supplies, Prepare to Evacuate, Prepare to Stay, Personal, Insurance, Financial, Assets, Final Planning

EVACUATION LIST AND CAR KIT

It's a good idea to be on the same page with your family when planning for an emergency. Review these concepts every few months as we all can be forgetful.

EVACUATION LIST:

When disaster strikes the last thing you want to be thinking about is what to grab. Fill out this grab list and tape near the exits to your home so you won't have to figure out what to grab during a crisis.

➡ 72 hour kits

➡ Emergency binder

➡ Photos

➡ Journals

➡

➡

➡

➡

➡

➡

➡

➡

CONSIDER MAKING A SEPARATE GRAB LIST FOR EACH FAMILY MEMBER. THEN EACH MEMBER WILL KNOW EXACTLY WHAT TO GRAB

CAR KIT:

In case you need to leave in a hurry, or get stuck in your car, a main focus on being prepared for "evacuation" is to have a well-stocked car.

✓ Water (a case of bottles would be excellent)

✓ 72 hour kit food, high calorie meal bars, snacks

✓ Cash (small bills and include some change)

✓ Diapers/Wipes if you have kids

✓ Emergency blankets/hand warmers

✓ Jumper cables

✓ Car shovel/pick

✓ Pocket knife

✓ First aid kit

✓ Radio

✓ Package of batteries (for flashlight and radio)

✓ Toilet paper roll

✓ Spare clothes for small children

✓ Coffee can heater

✓ Flash light

IF YOU HAVE A BABY, ALWAYS HAVE YOUR DIAPER BAG STOCKED. YOU NEVER KNOW WHEN YOU MAY NEED TO GRAB IT AND GO.

Last Minute Ways To Prepare

When disaster is about to strike, sometimes you will have advanced notice, sometimes you won't. Weather reports will often forecast a large hurricane; however, earthquakes will usually come unexpectedly. Should you find yourself in harm's way with time to prepare, here are some suggestions of things you could do to weather the storm.

1. Fill your gas tank.
2. Have a 72 hour kit for every person in your family.
3. Have cash in your 72 hour kits because if electricity is out bank ATM's won't work.
4. Turn your fridge and freezer to a colder setting & if you lose power keep the doors closed as much as possible.
5. If you have extra space in your freezer, take containers or zip-loc bags full of water and fill in the extra space.
6. Charge all your electronic devices and keep them charged in case you lose power.
7. Keep a list of emergency numbers handy, along with family members' phone numbers. Write them down if you only have them stored in your phone.
8. Have an emergency escape plan from your home and make sure all family members know it and know where to meet.
9. Clean out your gutters before the storm comes and make sure that the storm drains on your street are clear from all the fall foliage.
10. Check your sump pumps.
11. Be ready to help your neighbors.
12. Get batteries.
13. Get a radio so you know what's going on.
14. Board up your windows. Stay away from windows.
15. Have everyone sleep in the same room so you can keep tabs on them.
16. Make a few meals and snacks that will last without power.
17. Make sure to have a non-electric can opener.
18. Have lots of non-perishables on hand.
19. Have enough food and litter for your pets.
20. Have an emergency binder with all important paperwork ready to go.
21. Have your prescriptions filled.
22. If you have a gas grill, make sure you have a full tank of propane.
23. Do your laundry now, so you have clothes that are dry and clean.
24. Make sure you have a car charger for your cell phone.
25. If you have a fireplace that you can use to cook in, have a supply of wood.
26. Check with your elderly neighbors, and family members to make sure they are prepared or invite them over.
27. Find your glasses so you don't have to deal with contacts in an emergency.

28. You can use your water heater for extra water too. Just shut off the intake valve so that you aren't bringing in contaminated water and use the spigot in the front to dispense water.
29. Get some battery-powered fans for when your air conditioning doesn't function.
30. Keep items you don't want damaged by water in the dishwasher as it is waterproof.
31. Have glow sticks on hand for little ones, especially at bedtime.
32. Have a rain barrel to collect water you can use to flush toilets.
33. Get hand sanitizer and wet wipes to wash with.
34. Improvise an emergency toilet with a bucket lined with a biodegradable bag and some sawdust or cat litter to cover the contents after each use.
35. Be careful of carbon monoxide when using gas heaters/stoves or candles.
36. Take pictures of every room and closet in your house – it makes a huge difference if you have to deal with insurance companies. Keep these in a safe place.
37. Consider filling large containers (the big 40-gal Rubbermaid totes) from the tub spigot, and storing them in the tub. Cover all bins/tubs of water to keep kids and pets safe.
38. Get solar outdoor lights, you can use olive oil in jars with wicks as well.
39. Pick up a solar phone charger then you will still have power for your cell phone.
40. If you have a good old fashioned plug-in land line phone and socket this will serve you better than a cell phone.
41. Refill dish soap/laundry soap/ hand soap bottles back up slowly with water, you then have a easy bottles filled for light cleaning, and easy rinsing.
42. If you have to use a gas-powered generator, make sure to have extra fuel on hand; just be very careful where you put it, and be mindful of your local laws on how much you can have on hand at one time.
43. Don't forget to pay attention to fire prevention. Have your extinguisher handy.
44. A chainsaw is good for clearing fallen trees. Only use one if you have prior experience. The aftermath of a storm is not the time to be learning how to use it.
45. Anyone with an oxygen tank – make certain you have 1) a travel tank 2) a generator or means to operate your home device 3) notified health officials of your scheduled location during and after a hurricane.
46. Have books and other non-electric entertainment like board games ready for everyone (and flashlights or lanterns for when it gets dark).
47. Have canning lids on hand so you can can meat if freezer defrosts. Use either a wood/coal stove or a gas range. Have the jars sterilized in the dishwasher ready.
48. Use silicon caulking to seal a stopper in the bathtub before filling it. Lock the door as a safety measure for kids that may climb in.
49. Prepare a list of things you would need to grab in case you need to evacuate.
50. Turn OFF the TV! If you want to keep updated check for updates then turn it off. The constant hype will stress you and your children out.

Emergency Heat Sources

Keeping warm is essential for survival. Hypothermia, loss of body heat is very dangerous and can lead to loss of body parts and even death. Wet conditions quickly increase the loss of body heat. Here are some heat sources:

Dry (preferably wool) clothing: If you get wet from rain, snow or sweat, change into clothing that is dry. Wet clothing loses its insulation value and extracts body heat much faster than dry clothing. Wool clothing and blankets are preferred. Cotton clothing, particularly denim, retains water. Wool is insulating, water resistant, and keeps your body warm even if wet.

Hats and mittens (preferably gloves): Covering your head is vital as you can lose up to 80% of your body heat through your head. A knitted wool stocking hat is good.

Insulated boots or shoes: Feet can be kept warm by wearing wool socks. Wear two pairs if your shoes are large enough. A towel can also be wrapped over shoes and duct-taped on.

Layered clothing: Several thin layers of loose-fitting clothing retain body heat and can be removed easily if body starts to perspire and/or you are chilling. Water & wind resistant outer clothing with a hood. Also, use a scarf or towel to cover your mouth to keep cold air from your lungs.

Sleeping bags: Two or more people huddled together inside two sleeping bags zipped together will be warmer than each in separate sleeping bags. A smaller bag can also be placed inside a larger-sized one.

Car heater: If trapped in your car during a snowstorm, run the heater 10 minutes every hour. Make sure the exhaust pipe is not blocked by snow and open one window a crack to allow ventilation.

Mylar blankets or emergency bags: Good in wind or rain. Put a wool blanket between you and the Mylar blanket, if possible.

Rice or bean-filled packs: You can use socks filled with rice/beans and tied shut as heating pads. Heat the packs/socks in a fire or coals. They will maintain heat for a period of time. Rocks or bricks can also be heated thoroughly, then carefully wrapped in towels or newspapers.

Insulated clothing: Leaves, newspaper, straw, etc. (stuffed between two layers of clothing). Tie your shoe laces around the cuffs of your pants to hold material in. If you are trapped in a car during a snowstorm, use the stuffing from the seat cushions.

Plastic garbage bag: This can be worn as a rain jacket or can insulate the body if stuffed with dry leaves or grass.

Ways to Keep Cool with No Power

Getting overheated can often be just as dangerous (or more dangerous) than being too cold. Heat exhaustion and heat stroke can be major concerns. We are used to having air conditioners, swamp coolers, or electric fans to help combat hot summers. But what can you do when the power is out? Here are fifty ideas for ways to stay cool.

1. Wear light-colored clothing, dark clothes absorb heat
2. Use a damp cloth to wet face, arms and legs
3. Find a cool breeze to sit in (especially after getting wet)
4. Make a paper fan and fan yourself
5. Hang out in the basement of your home
6. Install attic vents to release the hot air that rises
7. Sleep on the porch between wet sheets
8. Relax during the hottest hours, do heavy chores/cooking at morning and night
9. Do your canning and cooking outdoors
10. Take an afternoon nap
11. Use a buckwheat pillow, it won't hold on to your body heat
12. Close all blinds and window coverings (don't let the sun in)
13. Open all the windows at night to let cool air in
14. Lie down on the floor in the lowest level of your house
15. Keep a window open upstairs to pull hot air up and out
16. Wet your hair
17. Put white sheets over furniture, it will reflect heat instead of absorb it
18. Wrap a wet towel around your neck
19. Find shade trees to sit under
20. Take cool baths
21. Make sure your home is well insulated, it will keep the heat out
22. Drink lots of fluids
23. Use a spray bottle and spray yourself down
24. Hang wet sheets in open windows that have a cross breeze
25. Keep babies in a light onesie (not naked) for when you hold them
26. Dip feet in cool water
27. Keep your body covered (in cool clothes) to shade it from the sun
28. Don't wear polyester, it makes you sweat
29. Sit still, moving around makes you hotter
30. Make recipes using mint/peppermint to cool the body
31. Brush mint against the skin to cool you down
32. Wear loose-fitting skirts
33. Use battery-powered fans
34. Put wet rags over a battery-powered fan to make a cooler breeze

35. Give the kids squirt guns and have a water fight
36. Buy some evaporative cooling bandanas
37. Eat cold meals
38. Eat spicy foods, they increase perspiration which cools down the body
39. Buy some cooling towels/cloths
40. Wear a large-brimmed hat to shade your face
41. Spray your house down with a water hose for a temporary cool down
42. Keep ice packs in your freezer and then use them for relief
43. Wear minimal clothing (if appropriate)
44. Use silk or satin sheets and pillowcases, they feel cooler
45. Hang up bedding in cool areas of the house or shade during the day
46. Get a waterbed, it will absorb heat and feel cool on hot nights
47. Build porch awnings to provide shade
48. Have a generator to plug in electric fans
49. Make a homemade air conditioner or swamp cooler if you have a generator
50. GO SWIMMING!

Emergency Sanitation Kits

SANITATION KIT CONTENTS:
In a plastic tote with a lid, store the following items:
- Two 5- or 6-gallon plastic buckets with tight-fitting lids
- Two toilet seats that attach to the buckets
- Toilet paper, paper towels
- Pre-washed and dried flannel, cut into squares, to use if toilet paper is not available
- Hand wipes, hand sanitizer and hand soap
- 13-gallon trash bags (to line toilets)
- 33-gallon trash bags (to dispose of smaller, used bags and other trash)
- Three spray bottles (for hydrogen peroxide, white vinegar, and bleach)
- Hydrogen peroxide, white vinegar, borax and or bleach
- Essential oils and/or sprays for odor control
- Small funnel to fill bottles
- Super Sorb or other absorbent material
- Shovel
- Heavy gloves (for digging), disposable gloves (for cleaning)
- Face masks
- Copy of this sheet of instructions, stored in a plastic sheet protector
- Empty plastic jug (the kind you keep in the fridge) to hold water for hand washing

EMERGENCY TOILETS:
- Have 2 toilets—one for liquid waste and one for solid waste
- Place plastic liners in each toilet. You should double-line the toilet for solid waste.
- When the toilet is not in use, be sure to place a tight lid on top of the toilet
- In the toilet for urine, sprinkle one tablespoon of Super Sorb. It will decrease odors and absorb two gallons of fluid, turning it into a gel for easy clean-up and disposal.
- In the toilet for solid waste, sprinkle Borax, or use one part bleach to four parts water. These solutions will decrease odors, disinfect, and stop the spread of disease.
- Wash your hands after each use by using soap and water.
- Use 1/4 cup of bleach in a quart of water to disinfect surfaces; or for less toxic chemicals, use undiluted hydrogen peroxide in a spray bottle and undiluted white vinegar in a separate spray bottle. Spray one after the other on surfaces that need to be disinfected, then wipe off with a paper towel. Make sure you do not mix bleach and vinegar (only use them separately).

WASTE DISPOSAL:
Check with your local health department for their plans regarding waste disposal before a disaster. The following instructions are given by the Southwest Utah Public Health Department but your area may require something different: "Bury garbage and human waste to avoid the spread of disease by rats and insects. Dig a pit two to three feet deep and at least fifty feet downhill or away from any well, spring, or water supply." After dumping waste in the hole, sprinkle lime and then soil over the top to protect from animals, hasten decomposition, and decrease odors. We recommend using biodegradable waste bags to reduce the amount of garbage you are burying. Protect yourself by wearing gloves and a face mask.

Emergency Kits for Babies

If you have an infant or a toddler at home, consider including some or all of these items as you assemble your 72 hour kits for your family:

- **Instant formula.** Make sure to buy the kind you do not need to mix with water. Also, track expiration dates and rotate through them frequently.

- **5 small bottles for the formula.** You can fill them with purified water to provide extra drinking water in your kit.

- **Refrigerated bottle bag.** This is helpful in case you get the chance to warm up or cool down the formula. You can keep it at that temperature for around 4 hours.

- **Plenty of diapers.** The exact number needed depends on the age of your child. You may choose to do a mixture between disposable and cloth diapers.

- **A travel package of wipes.** These are great for washing as well. If you have space just store a full box of wet wipes.

- **Pacifiers**. Put in two just in case. If you're stressed the baby will probably be stressed and it's a comfort for them.

- **3 cotton/flannel wraps.** Make sure you have some for various temperatures.

- **Baby food.** Depending on the age of your child you will probably want to include some jars of baby food. Once your baby can eat mostly regular foods just pop these out.

- **Washcloths.** Store around 10 small ones.

- **Small comfort toys**. If your child has a specific toy or blanket that he/she really loves, try to grab that in an emergency. But if you can't, have a reasonable substitute that will help comfort the child in lieu of their favorite item.

- **Clothes** – and plenty of them! This is a tough one as babies grow so fast. As you swap out their closets to put in the next size of clothes, remember to do that in the disaster kit at the same time. Make sure to include clothes for all types of weather and include lots of spares.

- **Ziplock bags.** These work great for storing used diapers or anything else that is dirty, or clean for that matter.

- **Bulb nose syringe and saline.** Saline loosens mucous and the syringe sucks water/ mucous out of ears, nose, mouth, etc. You never know if you'll need one so it's great to keep in your kit.

- **Infant tylenol/motrin.** It never fails that kids get sick as soon as you are somewhere without your medicine. So this is a definite requirement for any child disaster kit.

- **Desitin** or other diaper rash cream and travel-sized baby powder if desired. The last thing you'd want in an emergency situation is a sore bum and nothing to treat it with.

Planning For Your Future

While this is a topic most people don't want to think about, it's very important to do at least some basic estate planning as soon as you have any assets and/or dependents. Here are some notes on basic estate planning. This is a starting point. Consult with your own professional on this topic as each family's needs and situations vary greatly.

BENEFITS OF ESTATE PLANNING:

- Avoid having your assets tied up in probate
- Clear directions on what will happen to your children should you and your spouse both pass away
- Beneficiaries can pay less inheritance tax
- Allows you to make decisions, rather than the courts
- Peace of mind in knowing things are taken care of

CREATE A WILL:

A will is the foundation of your estate planning. Without a will the courts will decide what happens to your children and your assets and your family that is left behind could be in for a mess. Your will should include the following items:

- Nominate a guardian for any children you have
- List your assets and how you want them distributed
- Name an executor of your estate to take care of fulfilling your wishes

A few things to consider:
- Beneficiaries on life insurance policies and financial accounts will take precedence over a will, so make sure they are all updated appropriately.
- Everyone that has assets should have a will.
- Review your will each year, modify it should any major life changes occur such as the death of a beneficiary, addition of new beneficiaries, major changes in financial situation, etc.
- Don't hide your will in a safe deposit box. Keep a copy somewhere your family can easily find it.

LIVING WILLS:

Having a living will allows you to decide whether or not you want to remain on artificial life support when there is no chance of recovery. It relieves your family of the burden of having to make that decision. This is a very good thing to have.

DURABLE POWER OF ATTORNEY:

A durable power of attorney allows you to name someone of your choice to handle your affairs in the event that you become unable to do so. You can specify what those circumstances are.

Powerless Cooking Stoves/Ovens

MAKE YOUR OWN #10 CAN STOVE:

A cheap and easy way to build a portable stove is by using a #10 can, cutting out holes for ventilation and placing wires through it to hold various sizes of pots. You can make #10 can stoves packed with fuels as gifts.

PRO: FREE to make
CON: Not all that efficient or sturdy (you will end up using more fuel)

CUBE STOVE:

The Cube stove is made of durable aluminized steel with an electrostatic surface which reflects heat better than stainless steel or other comparable surfaces. It can be used in 7 different positions to accommodate different needs, such as cooking fast or slow, or cooking in a large pot or small cup.

PRO: Small, durable, reusable, very inexpensive
CON: Doesn't fold down flat like the Firebox

FIREBOX STOVE:

Firebox 5" Folding Campfire Stove: "The most portable, versatile, easy to use cooking stove ever." It's a thin, portable campfire and multi-fuel stove with a 5" combustion chamber that burns very efficiently. Simply place combustible fuels in the Firebox and ignite from the top or bottom through the fire grate.

PRO: Very efficient, will conserve fuel, folds down into a thin flat stove
CON: Costs more than the free or cheap options

VOLCANO STOVE:

The Volcano Grill's unique heating chamber channels the heat upwards towards your food, instead of wasting fuel by expelling heat out the sides and bottom. You can use the Volcano with a variety of fuels, and cook with pots and pans, grills, woks, or dutch ovens. Perfect for camping and/or emergency preparedness.

PRO: Can use a variety of fuel such as propane, charcoal, Insta fire. You can grill, bake, fry, and more
CON: This is a heavier, larger stove. Not meant for compact backpacking situations

MAKE YOUR OWN CARDBOARD BOX OVEN:

You can build a cheap oven for baking bread or any other foods using an apple box or other large cardboard box. You wrap the box in aluminum foil and cut some ventilation holes at the bottom. You cook in it using charcoal at whatever temperature you desire.

PRO: Virtually FREE to make
CON: Not all that efficient or sturdy (you will end up using more fuel)

MAKE YOUR OWN PIZZA BOX OVEN:

You can make a solar oven using a pizza box wrapped in foil and propped open to reflect the sun. Temperatures do not get very hot so it works more like a slow cooker or just to heat up leftovers. Not ideal for long term cooking but great in a pinch.

PRO: Virtually FREE to make
CON: Doesn't get very hot, long cooking times, not very durable

HELIUS ROCKET STOVE:

The Helius is a very efficient rocket stove that has the ability to regulate the temperature based on how much fuel you are using. This plus its heavy durability make it one of the only stoves of it's kind that can be pressure canned on. This can be very useful in an emergency situation where you need to hurry and can meat or other freezer foods.

PRO: Uses multiple fuels, ability to pressure can, heavy duty
CON: Fairly expensive, heavy so not portable, must be used outside

HERC TEA-LIGHT CANDLE OVEN:

Available in two sizes this is the only oven on the market that allows you to bake like normal inside your house with no electricity. It is highly efficient and inexpensive to cook with since it uses only tea-light candles to heat clay plates and heat up the oven.

PRO: Able to use indoors, can bake in a 9x13 pan, inexpensive fuel, safe
CON: A little tricky to assemble, higher-priced, must have specific fuel

ALL-AMERICAN SUN OVEN:

ASun-Oven should be a staple for everyone's powerless cooking arsenal due to the fact that it uses a free unlimited fuel source. Cook with the power of the sun for as many meals as possible to conserve fuel. They are very versatile, allowing you to cook a variety of foods, and they are built to last.

PRO: Uses NO fuel, can bake, grill, boil, re-heat, dehydrate, etc.
CON: Not usable indoors, usage is limited to sunny or partially sunny days

Emergency Fuel

WOOD:

Raw, dry wood is a very good source of fuel although it often becomes wet and unusable in a disaster. It is also good for heating so it's a valuable fuel to store, even though it takes up a lot of space.

Indoor cooking: Wood-burning stove or open fireplace (make sure they are properly vented to outside)

Outdoor cooking: Open pit fire or Volcano Grill

Storage limitations: In rural areas wood may be readily available at a relatively low cost but local permits may be necessary. In some areas wood may not be as available and storage areas are limited.

Shelf life: Virtually unlimited as long as kept dry and covered.

1 Month Supply (3 meals a day): About 150-300 lbs depending on wood type and how you are cooking.

PROPANE:

Available in several sizes ranging from 1 pound to very large containers and is a good source for both heat and cooking.

Indoor cooking: When using propane to cook indoors you can only use a natural gas stove that has been adapted for propane use. Without proper alterations it is extremely dangerous to use inside.

Outdoor cooking: Barbecue grill, small camp stoves, or Volcano Grill

Storage limitations: Never store propane indoors, or in an attached garage. It should be stored in a location that gets little to no direct sunlight and has ventilation such as a storage shed or unattached garage. Limitations on amounts you are allowed to store generally apply due to its explosive nature. Check with your local fire department for specific storage restrictions in your area. (For some states it is 30 pounds per household)

Shelf life: Most containers have a "use by date", they need to be re-certified 12 years from that date and every 10 years after that.

1 Month Supply (3 meals a day): 2 standard bbq grill tanks, about 35-40 pounds of propane.

COAL/CHARCOAL:

Coal can be a good source of heat and charcoal is great for outdoor cooking. Both are fairly easy to store without safety concerns.

Indoor cooking: A coal-burning stove can be used for "one-pot cooking" with proper ventilation. Charcoal should not be used indoors.

Outdoor cooking: Charcoal can be used for dutch oven cooking, in a barbecue grill, or in a Volcano Grill

Storage limitations: Large amounts are needed but it is easy to calculate how much you need to store. Must be kept dry.

Shelf life: Charcoal and coal can be stored indefinitely in dry locations indoors or outdoors.

1 Month Supply (3 meals a day): Approximately 120 lbs of coal.

INSTA-FIRE:

Insta-Fire is a safe, simple, and versatile fire-starting product. You can use it to light campfires, prepare charcoal briquettes, or as a safe and reliable fuel source for cooking or heating in emergency situations.

Indoor cooking: Insta-fire can be used in a wood-burning stove or open fireplace. The key is to have proper ventilation.

Outdoor cooking: Works fantastic by itself in a Volcano Grill, can also be used in a #10 can stove, open fire pit, or directly on the ground (even on snow).

Storage limitations: None. May be stored indoors, next to food, in basements or attics, or outdoors.

Shelf life: 30 year shelf life.

1 Month Supply (3 meals a day): About one 5 gallon bucket (1 cup used per meal).

BUTANE:

Comes in small canisters usually about 8 ounces. Can be purchased in cases of 12.

Indoor cooking: Butane is a safe clean fuel that can be used indoors.

Outdoor cooking: Your butane stove can also be used outdoors if you don't want to heat up your kitchen.

Storage limitations: Butane is safe to store indoors and there are no storage limitations as it is not combustable. Butane should not be stored outdoors if you have extreme weather temperatures. Safe storage temperature is between 32 and 125 degrees Fahrenheit.

Shelf life: Butane cans typically have a shelf life of about 8 years.

1 Month Supply (3 meals a day): About 15 of the 8 ounce cans (depending on cook times).

READY FUEL GEL:

A gel that comes in small foil packets inside a large cardboard box.

Indoor cooking: The ReadyFuel gel is safe to use indoors. Put it on a metal surface to avoid any fire hazards.

Outdoor cooking: ReadyFuel can be used outdoors but it does not light well in windy conditions.

Storage limitations: ReadyFuel can be stored inside or outside with no limitations.

Shelf life: ReadyFuel has a 30+ year shelf life.

1 Month Supply (3 meals a day): 120 fuel packets will boil 30 gallons of water or give you 4 cooking opportunities per day.

PLEASE NOTE: There are many safety concerns with the proper storage and usage of cooking fuels. Take necessary precautions when storing fuels.

BABYSTEP 1: SHELVES

INTRODUCTION:

★ There are a wide variety of shelf options available. Determine the amount you feel comfortable spending and consider what will best suit your needs.

★ Options to store canned goods and other pantry foods:

- Build Your Own - Cheap & offers the most flexibility, but time-intensive
  - ‣ Try making some rotating racks of cardboard (see inside this section)
  - ‣ Find other plans online
  - ‣ Cardboard shelves are also available

- Inexpensive metal or plastic shelving - A cheap and easy way to get started, shelves may not be as durable.

- Higher quality metal shelves - Heavy duty hardware store shelves should have no problem with bowing or collapsing under heavy weights. We recommend the Gorilla Shelves you can often find at Costco.

- Deluxe Can Rotation System - Most expensive option, but very convenient for easily rotating through foods.

★ Start with one set of shelves and add more as your food storage grows. Plastic may be better than metal for storing heavier items (cheap metal shelves tend to bow in the middle).

★ Adjustable shelf heights help you store different types and sizes of foods and cans.

★ Clear a space near your shelves for 5 gallon buckets/water containers/etc. Cover the floor with old carpet or pallets to avoid storing directly on concrete.

★ Don't let small spaces intimidate you – it can be done if you decide to commit yourself and be creative.

INSIDE THIS SECTION:

Small Spaces Storage Solutions
Rotating Rack Instructions
Rotating Rack Diagram
Can and Bucket Storage

Small Spaces Storage Solutions

At Food Storage Made Easy, our blog readers came together and shared ideas for storing food in small spaces. The results were incredible! Here are some of the best ones.

BEDROOMS:

We put short bookshelves in our son's closet and used them for food storage. Since his clothes were small they fit great over the top of the shelves. We also stacked boxes of #10 cans in the ends of the closets. Just make sure the boxes are labeled with what's in them and put the things you will need to get into most often on the top or it can be a real pain to find things.
-Ellie

Store cans on their sides under a twin bed. Line them up in rows of their category (fruit, veggies, tuna, etc.). When you purchase cans place under the left side of the bed. When you need a can for meal preparation pull it from the right side.
-Shaela

My husband and I decided to convert one of the bedrooms into our food storage room. We took the smallest of the three, bought heavy duty shelves from Costco and ordered a Shelf Reliance storage system for our canned goods. The closet in our food storage room holds our wheat, powdered milk, and bottled water. We also raised our bed up, and have rolling totes underneath for additional storage.
-Samantha

You can get wide, shallow plastic bins that have wheels on them for rolling under your bed. These are great for storing cans of food since they are about as deep as a can. You can easily pull them out for food rotation purposes as well.
-Amanda

Don't forget all the wonderful storage underneath your beds! You could house cases of canned goods or extra paper goods - anything really! Lots of space, you just have to remember what is under there and keep rotating if it is anything perishable.
-Julie

Boxes fit perfectly under my children's beds. That not only gives me extra storage space, but it prevents the build-up of toys and clothes and candy wrappers that otherwise get stuffed under the beds.
-Marilee

I have wheat boxes behind my bed headboard against the wall, in a layer under my daughter's mattress (she doesn't have a frame or boxspring), and under the TV (that layer is covered with a blanket). We hardly notice they're around. I also have water stored under my bed (I used to store it under the couch – that's a great place to store extra diapers, too).
-America

KITCHENS:

Buy some of the heavy duty Velcro from any store. The stuff that's about two to three inches across. Put one side on the back of a pantry, or cabinet, then attach pieces of the other side to your spices. Easy spice rack on the back of the door for almost nothing. Works even with the really big Costco spice jars. We have a couple rows of this, keeping the spices organized, and easy to use.
-Jayce

Inside the door of our pantry and the converted coat closet hang a pantry door shelf that hooks over the top of the door. The one in the pantry holds my 50 or more spices. The second row from the bottom holds my nonstick sprays and Crisco. The bottom shelf holds all my pancake syrups and a big bag of Krusteez.
- Maggie

Under our kitchen sink it was just our trash and a mess of plastic bags. To get that organized he took all the plastic grocery bags. We kept our small stash of dishwasher soap on the side and near it we kept our small garbage can. Then with all the left over space under there... after cleaning the space really well, my husband put our case of Tomato Soup, Spaghettios, and Progresso soups.
-Maggie's Husband

If your kitchen has a breakfast bar that is too tall for eating (approx. 46 inches) then find someone (husband, a family friend, or pay someone) to custom make shallow cupboards underneath the counter. If they are made with a wood to match your kitchen cabinets then it should be a nice useful addition to your kitchen.
-Maggie

I use Turn Table Spice Racks to keep my spaces organized and easy to rotate. It ends up taking less space because I can pile spices all the way to the back but still have access to them. I also put my baking goods in plastic bins so I can easily take out all my ingredients at once when I bake, again it keeps things packed away in tighter spaces and makes cooking more fun.
-Crystal

CLOSETS:

Create false bottoms in your closets! Clear everything out of the bottom of your chosen closet. Fill that space with either #10 cans or a couple of cases of canned goods. Cut a piece of plywood (or have it cut for you!) to size and place on top of the cans. Now, use your closet as you normally would!
-Danielle

We converted our coat closet to a little storage room (we kept the coats in our regular closet). We used boards and #10 cans to "build" shelves and it was amazing how much stuff we were could put in there.
-Gwen and Melissa

After struggling to find places for our storage, I got the idea to convert our coat closet into a pantry. The closet wasn't in our kitchen but had lots of space that wasn't being utilized. Our coats and other items were moved to our bedroom closets. My husband added shelves and removed the closet rod.
-Denise

I also repurposed a canvas sweater holder that hung in the closet for boxes of pasta, cereal and crackers in my front 'coat' closet - those that didn't fit in the tiny kitchen cupboards. I converted the broom closet into a kitchen pantry (it was about 15 inches deep) with some shelf brackets and wood cut at Home Depot.
-CTD

We converted our coat closet into another food pantry. Since this closet is not directly in the kitchen and it is carpeted we store our #10 cans, case lot sales items, and items purchased in bulk that we have a lot of. I stock my main pantry from this converted coat closet. The coat closet also had a built in shelf above the rod, so that shelf is used for unopened boxes of food like our case of 48 cans of Tuna and our 72 hours kits (grab and go kits near a door exiting the house).
-Maggie

I have a one year supply of fruit that I home canned. My mother had tons of milk crates from years ago, and we filled them up and now they are stacked high in my closest and under my hanging clothes. That's where my fruit is. I have learned to put things in places that can be hidden so it doesn't look like I have food all over my house. The kids closets are stacked high with boxes of # 10 cans.
-Alisha

CREATIVE SPACES:

I live in a manufactured home (no basement) with a large master bathroom that has a corner "garden" tub. The side access panels are held on with velcro. I store my laundry supplies in the dead space under the tub.
-Mary Lou

What I'm planning on doing is curtaining off two feet or so along one wall of the dining room (Ikea has curtain rails you can mount on the ceiling) and putting all my food storage on shelves behind it.
-Cathie

In one house there was a space under the stairwell and we cut an opening in there and put a door so we could store things there. It was quite small, but functional. We've always looked around at wherever we were living for available space.
-Gwen

The laundry/utility room often has extra space above the washer and dryer that can be used. Even if you don't want to put food there, it works for storing toilet paper, dish soap, shampoos, etc.
-Gwen

We took sheets of 2 inch blueboard and made a 4x10 food storage room at the end of our very small living room. Made a door out of duct tape/blueboard.
-Janet

You can put organizers under your sink that are adjustable and can fit around all the pipes. It's a great way to have shelves under that awkward space. I also put racks directly on the cupboards to hold different kinds of plastic wrap, aluminum foil etc.
-Crystal

FURNITURE:

This is an amazing idea that we received multiple times, it's about creating a shelving system that acts as a table behind a sofa. It's so neat! http://www.youtube.com/watch?v=FCnXfO7YMfk
-Ruth, Mary Lou, Linda

These are things my mom did, she put wheat in buckets, using one on both sides she would put a piece of cut plywood across it and make a shelf. We got to put contact paper of our choice on the wood and the bucket to decorate or rooms with and she would stack them 2 high. They make great book shelves. Now they have such great things to decorate, you could go wild with it, maybe faux painting some to look like marble pillars? You could even use the shelves to put other food stuffs on and put a curtain or sheet in front to make a make-shift "cupboard".
-Lorie

I sewed a liner for a big basket I had (like a big bag). Then I was able to put extra oatmeal boxes, crackers etc in it. I put a round table top (the kind you screw legs on) on it and used it as an end table. The bag liner hid the contents....When I moved to a bigger 1 bedroom apartment that same basket was used to store all the extra laundry detergent and dryer sheets I would stock up on at sales, soap and shampoo too - since I didn't have a linen closet.
-CTD

Knowing we needed space to store food and some casual seating, we made 18" cubes with hinged lids. Added casters on the bottom, padded seating on top. Inside it held about 4 cases worth of canned veggies, soup, etc. We made 3 of these boxes, then made a table to store them under. On the table we used decorative items: a nice looking binder for our storage records, a pretty box that held recipes for our storage foods, another box held cards with helpful hints. A lamp and a phone rounded out the decoration s.
-Lou

One year when we lived in an apartment my in-laws gave us a big wicker chest for Christmas. We put it in our living room and filled it with cans. We were amazed at how many cans could fit in it. We had a futon in our living room and we hid soda bottles filled with water behind the futon.
-Ellie

The food storage boxes from the church canneries (the kind that hold six #10 cans each) fit very nicely between the wall and my couches. Every piece of furniture in my living room and family room has food storage boxes behind it. I stack them about 3 boxes tall, and then extend them as long as the couch. It leaves just the perfect amount of space between the wall and the furniture -- nobody would guess there was anything back there. Those boxes also can be stacked to form a table -- my telephone sits on one such table. It's just boxes with a cloth over them.
-Marilee

SHELVING:

I bought 2 book shelves at a garage sale - asking price $40 each, bought both for $25. They have been a great addition for storage! I have the shelves stored in my office, but when you look down the hall from our main living area you don't see them.
-Marilyn's daughter

I like the slender boxes that 3 - 1 gal water comes in for regular cans-the can fit nicely laying sideways (2 rows)- the box is slender to put in room and has the concept of the rotating method for the higher priced shelves
-Linda

WHOLE HOUSE:

I use one place for one food group. Like canned meats, chili, and soup for under the bed, canned veggies on top of cupboards, and fruits under end tables with fabric draped over it. Also if your filling cabinet isn't full, fill it up with boxed items, or put food in a crawl space or attic well sealed. Keep a detailed inventory handy so you don't forget how much & what you have (for me it's outta' sight, outta' mind). Post your list on the inside of a cupboard so it's tucked away. Also, tape a pen or pencil on a string, or velcro (my favorite) a pen next to it. That way, when you're in a hurry, you can mark it instead of trying to remember what you took later.
-Nicole

We have used the top space in closets, a drawer in a bench, under beds (even propped the beds up on blocks so the food would fit underneath), lined every closet with food and/or water. Pull a dresser or couch away from the wall a couple of feet and you can fit lots of cans or buckets behind it where they won't be seen too easily. We put food in the mylar pouches in the rolly boxes that go under beds and in giant 55 gal metal drums in the carport (the drums sealed so the insects/rodents/critters weren't able to get to our food. Make a table with a board on top of a couple of cases of canned goods and cover it with a cloth. I've stacked 2 liter pop bottles of water horizontally between my filing cabinet and the wall. I'm also okay with the fact that my house doesn't look professionally decorated—it's "disguise the food" décor!
-Angela

Rotating Rack Instructions

STEP 1:

Look at the shelf diagram {found on page 67} and determine what size of shelf you want to make.

STEP 2:

Take a large cardboard box and measure out the pieces. The easiest way with the least cuts and gluing is to measure for the entire length of both sides and back. For the vegetable can, this would be a total of 31-1/8" by 10". A carpenter's square is ideal to measure, mark, and cut, but any ruler will work.

STEP 3:

Cut out all of your pieces using an exacto-knife or other sharp blade or even some scissors. If you used a long piece for the side/back pieces then you'll need to bend the side pieces in to the right shape. You can use the carpenter's square (or ruler) to help bend a straight line.

STEP 4:

Take the side and back pieces (or the one large piece) and make sure the can fits properly. If not, back to the measuring board! Mark the shelf lines on the side pieces so that you will know where the shelves need to go when you glue them on. All measurements will vary with the size of unit you're building, so make sure to get them right!

STEP 5:

Glue the pieces together. Hot glue is fabulous for this step! With the big piece open, glue each shelf in place. Then glue them to the back. Don't forget to put in your wedge, and make sure a can will still pass between the wedge and shelf 2. The other side is the hardest part, because the glue may start to set before all the pieces are in place. After the other side is on, take the front pieces, with the edges bent in ¾, and glue them into place, one side at a time.

STEP 6:

Cut some little notches out of the side pieces near the bottom to enable you to pull the cans out more easily. At this point you can paint the whole thing with white latex paint if you want to strengthen the shelves.

Rotating Rack Diagram

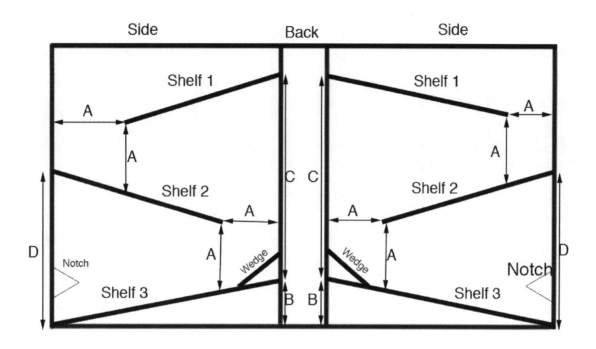

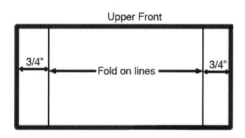

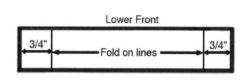

Measurements

Description	Fruit Can 4 1/2 x 3 3/8	Vegetable Can 4 3/8 x 3	Evap Milk Can 4 x 3	Soup Can 4 x 2 5/8
Sides	F 9¼ x B 10 x 11½	10 x 13	10 x 13	F 9 x B 10½ x 12
Back	5 ¼ x 9 ¼	5 1/8 x 10	4 5/8 x 10	4 3/8 x 10 ½
Shelf 1 & 2	5 1/8 x 8	5 x 9 ¾	4 ½ x 9 ¾	4 ¼ x 9 1/8
Bottom Shelf	5 1/8 x 11 5/8	5 x 13 1/8	4 ½ x 13 1/8	4 ¼ x 12 1/8
Upper Front	6 ¾ x 4 3/8	6 5/8 x 4 ¾	6 1/8 x 4 ¾	5 7/8 x 3 1/8
Lower Front	6 ¾ x 1 ¼	6 5/8 x 1 ¼	6 1/8 x 1 ¼	5 7/8 x 1 ¼
Wedge	5 1/8 x 2 1/8	5 x 2 1/8	4 ½ x 2 1/8	4 ¼ x 2 1/8
A	3 ½	3 ¼	3 ¼	2 ¾
B	¾	1 ¼	1 ¼	1 ¾
C	7 5/8	7 ¾	7 ¾	7 7/8
D	4 7/8	5 ¼	5 ¼	5 7/8

Can and Bucket Storage

When you are making plans for your shelving units, it's a good thing to consider what will be going on those shelves. Whether it's canned goods, #10 cans, or buckets, each take up different space.

Here are some benchmarks for how much food you may be packing in different size containers.

Food Item	#10 Can	5 Gallon Bucket
Wheat	5 lbs	37 lbs
White Flour	4.5 lbs	33 lbs
Cornmeal	4.3 lbs	33 lbs
Popcorn	5 lbs	37 lbs
Rolled Oats	2.5 lbs	20 lbs
White Rice	5.3 lbs	36 lbs
Spaghetti	3.1 lbs	30 lbs
Macaroni	3.1 lbs	21 lbs
Dried Beans	5.6 lbs	35 lbs
Lima Beans	5.4 lbs	35 lbs
Soy Beans	5 lbs	33 lbs
Split Peas	5 lbs	33 lbs
Lentils	5.5 lbs	33 lbs
White Sugar	5.7 lbs	35 lbs
Brown Sugar	4.42 lbs	33 lbs
Powdered Milk	3 lbs	29 lbs
Powdered Eggs	2.6 lbs	20 lbs

* Numbers come mainly from Thrive Life cans and buckets

BABYSTEP 2: WATER

INTRODUCTION:

★ Most sources recommend storing 1 gallon of water per person, per day, for 3-14 days. (Make sure to consider storing enough for pets as well).

★ Store water in "FOOD GRADE" or PETE plastic containers (stay away from milk jugs, but soda bottles are suitable). Most containers will say what kind of plastic it is on them.

★ Mylar bags stored in cardboard boxes are another option.

★ Store water away from too much light or heat, in cleaned and sanitized containers.

★ Do not use containers previously used to store non-food products.

★ Store water in multiple sizes of containers to suit different emergency needs.

★ Do not store containers directly on concrete. Place on cardboard or wood pallets.

★ Non-chlorinated water (most municipal water is chlorinated) should be treated with unscented liquid household chlorine bleach (5 to 6% sodium hypochlorite). Use this chart for appropriate amount to add to water.

Amount of Water	Amount of bleach to add to clear water	Amount of bleach to add to cloudy water
1 quart	2 drops	4 drops
1 gallon	8 drops	16 drops
5 gallons	1/2 teaspoon	1 teaspoon

★ Boiling is the safest way to clean water, however you can also use household liquid bleach to kill microorganisms.

★ Rotate your water storage at least once every year unless you use mylar bags or other options with longer shelf lives.

★ Alternate water sources include: Hot water heater tank, toilet tanks, water pipes, ice in freezer, canned food, rivers, streams, ponds and lake, snow and ice, rain water, etc.

INSIDE THIS SECTION:

Water Storage Containers
Water Rotation and Conservation
Water Filtration vs Purification

Water Storage Containers

Store 3-14 days worth of drinking water for your family. Store a minimum of 1 gallon per person per day. If you have a large family or a smaller home, this can prove to be a difficult task. If you have some solutions in place for purification/filtration your storage needs may be less. However, it is never a bad thing to have lots of actual water stored in case you don't have access to any water in an emergency. Here is a list of potential storage container options:

USED 2 LITER BOTTLES OR POP JUGS:

Pros:
• Essentially FREE if you buy them anyway or get from someone else
• Convenient size for smaller water emergencies
• Easy to store anywhere in the house

Cons:
• Must rotate every 6 months to 1 year
• Hard to clean out enough that the taste isn't a bit "off"
• Concern about bacteria if not cleaned out well enough

Best Used For:
• 72 Hour Kits
• People on a tight budget
• Small spaces storage solutions

STORE-BOUGHT WATER BOTTLES:

Pros:
• Great tasting, so it's ideal for drinking water
• Easy to rotate through the individual bottles
• Easy to store anywhere in the house

Cons:
• Must rotate every 6 months to 1 year
• Price per gallon can be fairly expensive
• Difficult to store in large quantities
• Bottles will freeze in winter, and chemicals can leach into them in severe heat, so not ideal for car kits in extreme conditions

Best Used For:
• 72 hour kits
• People concerned with taste of drinking water
• Small emergencies

SMALL WATER POUCHES OR WATER BOX CARTONS:

Pros:
• 5 year shelf life
• Awesome for 72 hour kits
• Water typically won't freeze in the pouches or small water boxes

Cons:
• Expensive storage method
• Not ideal for large quantities
• Not available in local stores everywhere

Best Used For:
• 72 Hour Kits
• Car kits

5/6 GALLON PLASTIC JUGS:

Pros:
• Better price per gallon
• More convenient size than large barrels
• Fairly easy to empty and rotate
• Easy to find in the camping section of most stores

Cons:
• Many of these jugs end up having problems with cracking and leaking so beware
• 5 or 6 gallon jugs can be heavy if you are trying haul them up and down stairs by yourself
• Must be rotated every 6 months to 1 year
• You can't stack them

Best Used For:
• Smaller storage spaces
• Tighter budgets

WATER BOX KITS (MYLAR BAGS INSIDE OF CARDBOARD BOXES):

Pros:
• Good price per gallon
• Stackable up to 3 boxes high
• Only have to rotate every 5 years

Cons:
• A little bit complicated to set them up and fill them
• Wasted space in your storage room above the stack of boxes
• Not very convenient for accessing small amounts of your water storage
• Not available in local stores everywhere

Best Used For:
• Larger quantities for people who don't like rotating
• Great for sliding under beds or sticking on closet shelves

WATER BRICKS:

Pros:
- 3.5 gallons per brick makes it more manageable than 5/6 gallon containers
- Stackable from floor to ceiling
- They are safe to freeze so can be stored outside
- Great size to stash under beds, in closets, etc.

Cons:
- A little more expensive per gallon
- Not available in local stores everywhere

Best Used For:
- Storage rooms where space is an issue
- Shorter term water emergencies for drinking and cooking
- People without considerable budget restraints

WATER BARRELS:

Pros:
- Best solution for storing lots of water
- Available in multiple sizes from 30 gallons up to 250 gallons
- With additives, can extend rotation needs to every 5 years
- Great use of floor space in a storage room with water barrel towers

Cons:
- Slightly difficult to fill and rotate
- Not very accessible when you have to actually use the water
- Not an ideal solution in small homes/storage areas and shouldn't be stored outside (garage is ok)

Best Used For:
- Longer term water shortages
- Large quantities of water storage

Remember, you will probably find that a combination of these storage containers works well for you.

Water Rotation and Conservation

With properly treated water stored in perfect conditions you may be able to get away with never rotating your water. However, it's usually better to be safe than sorry. Bacteria, algae, etc. can start to grow in your water making it very unpleasant (and unsafe) to drink. Store-bought water needs to be rotated by its "expiration date" because the plastic used for the containers can break down and/or start to leech chemicals into the water. If you re-use containers it is also very possible that there could be remnants of food/water left in the container that can be a contaminant to the water over time. Even if you are using brand new containers and purified water, there is always the chance that something from the air can get into your containers and cause the water to become contaminated.

HOW OFTEN TO ROTATE WATER:

There are many differing recommendations on how often you should rotate your water storage. Assuming you have properly stored your water, it is a good idea to check your water every six months. Make sure nothing is growing in it and that it is still drinkable. Unless you add a special additive (see below) it is recommended that you rotate your water once a year. Your water probably may still be ok if you go longer than that, but it is better to be on the safe side.

TIPS TO ROTATE LESS OFTEN:

Here are a few things that can help your water stay drinkable longer:
• Store in opaque containers to keep out light (dark green and blue are best)
• Store in a place that is dark and cool consistently
• Sterilize any containers you are storing water in before filling
• Treat your water with a special water treatment. The Aquamira Water Treatment combo can treat up to 60 gallons of water and they claim "When used according to instructions, and kept in a sealed container, treated water lasts 5 years"
• If you have a good water purifier you may choose to avoid rotating and just treat all water when the time comes to use it

WHAT TO DO WITH ROTATED WATER:

If you have hundreds of gallons of water stored, you want to make sure to be able to use the old water so you aren't wasting it. Some ideas for using your water are:
• Rotate in the spring and water your lawn and gardens with it
• Use it to flush your toilets
• Run several batches of laundry using stored water
• Wash your car with it
• Water house plants
• Purify it and use it for drinking/cooking
• Give your dog a bath

HOW TO IMPROVE WATER THAT HASN'T BEEN ROTATED:

If you haven't been diligent about rotating your water, all is not lost! Most often the biggest complaint is just the taste of the water. You can improve the taste by pouring the water back and forth between two containers a few times. This will aerate it and improve the taste. It's also a good idea to store some sort of drink mix like Tang, Crystal Light, Koolade, etc. if you have picky "drinkers". If you are worried about the safety of your water, you can always boil it to purify it. If you are conserving fuel or need to also filter out any particles, then have a good filter/purifier like a Berkey or Sawyer system on hand. The idea is to make sure you have a way to have clean and drinkable water in the case of an emergency.

WATER CONSERVATION:

In the case of a long term water shortage, there are many things to consider. Ideally you will have a filtration and purification method in place, and the ability to gather more water in case of a long term emergency, but this may not always be the case. Here are some tips on how to conserve the little water that you have or are able to collect:

- First, fill your water containers. We hear from so many people that they have containers that they just haven't gotten around to filling yet.
- Bathe in a large bucket or bin, and use bottles that have the types of tops that squirt. This will help with faster rinsing. Use the remaining water in the bucket for flushing toilets.
- Use coralite bath wipes, or baby wipes for quick bathing.
- Store some no-rinse shampoo and conditioner for hair.
- Have paper plates, plastic cups, and disposable tableware to use.
- Use recipes that mix most ingredients in one dish or pan to cut back on dish-washing.
- Store wet wipes and hand sanitizer to help clean up messes and wash hands.
- Tap into your water heater and toilet tanks for water if you run out of stored water.
- Wear your hair in ponytails, or wear hats when you can't wash your hair as frequently.
- If you have a swamp cooler that runs on water, make sure you have back-up cooling methods such as fans or wet rags to cool your body off during hotter weather.
- Fill liquid soap/detergent bottles with water and use for washing small load of dishes.
- Save water from cooking noodles or other foods to use for other things. Use water from canned vegetables.
- Don't wait until you are out of clean clothes to do laundry! If you're always on top of your laundry, hopefully if crisis hits you won't be stuck with a lot of laundry to do.
- If you have to do laundry get a bucket, put a little baking soda, a tad of water, plunge. No need to rinse with baking soda. Baking soda will eradicate smell too.
- Flush conservatively. Use water you previously used for bathing or washing dishes to flush the toilets.

Water Filtration vs. Purification

It's important to understand the difference between filtration and purification so that should you need to access water for a long term emergency, you will know how to properly treat your water. Depending on how contaminated your water is, a simple filter may be safe enough. But it is usually better to be on the safe side and fully purify all drinking water.

WATER FILTRATION:

Think of water filtration like a strainer. You have a filter with tiny holes in it which will block certain undesirable things from getting through. Any chunks of dirt, rocks, bugs, etc. will be filtered out. Most filters today will also do a good job at blocking protozoa (i.e. Cryptosporidium, Giardia) and bacteria (i.e. Salmonella, E. coli). However, viruses are so small that they will get through the holes in a regular filter. If you use a water "filter" it is a good idea to also purify the water once you have strained out the larger impurities.

WATER PURIFICATION:

Water purification makes water safe to drink but does not necessarily remove all undesirable elements from the water (large items such as dirt, rocks, etc.). Water can be purified by boiling it (for at least 3 minutes to kill everything), by using chemicals such as iodine or chlorine, by using UV, or by using special water purifiers that are rated to actually kill viruses (i.e. Enteric, Hepatitis A, Norovirus, Rotavirus).

Non-chlorinated water (most municipal water is chlorinated) should be treated with unscented liquid household chlorine bleach (5 to 6% sodium hypochlorite). Use this chart for appropriate amount to add to water.

Amount of Water	Amount of bleach to add to clear water	Amount of bleach to add to cloudy water
1 quart	2 drops	4 drops
1 gallon	8 drops	16 drops
5 gallons	1/2 teaspoon	1 teaspoon

FILTRATION/PURIFICATION COMBOS:

If you prefer to have one product that will both filter and purify your water here are two great ones. The Berkey Water Filter is very popular and it's great for both every day use and for emergency situations. There is also a product called AquaPail which works in a different way than the Berkey but is equally effective. It has an indefinite shelf life so you can store it and know that it is available in a long term water emergency.

BABYSTEP 3: 3 MONTH SUPPLY

INTRODUCTION:

★ Go through the five 3-month supply "questions to ask yourself" {found on page 77} to help you get started with the planning process.

★ Make a list of foods you eat on a regular basis and determine how much you would use in three months. Use the worksheets in this chapter to make your plan.

★ Gradually purchase these foods in bulk as they go on sale.

★ Combine sale prices with coupons for even more savings as you stock up.

★ Use and rotate these foods in all your daily cooking.

★ Constantly replenish the stocks of these foods as they go on sale again.

★ Don't forget to include non-food items in this step as well. Get at least a 3 month supply of necessities such as diapers, medications, toilet paper, toiletries, etc.

★ Benefits include: saving money by buying foods on sale, being prepared for "everyday emergencies", and having foods you normally eat in times of economic hardship or any other type of short-term emergency.

INSIDE THIS SECTION:

3 Month Supply: Questions to Ask Yourself
3 Month Supply Planning
Menu Plan
Inventory Sheet

3 Month Supply: Questions to Ask

When it comes to gathering a 3 month supply of food, it is common to get stuck on where to start. Ask yourself these questions, and as you do so you'll see a plan start to form.

WHY AM I BUILDING A 3 MONTH SUPPLY?

Are you storing a 3 month supply of food for a potential job loss? For a potential natural disaster? For meal planning purposes? Whatever it is that you are doing this for will influence how you go about planning, so first – decide – Why Am I Doing This?

WHAT KINDS OF FOODS DO I WANT TO INCLUDE?

Are you the type that thinks your 3 month plan can only have shelf stable pantry items? Do you think fridge and freezer foods count in your 3 month plan? Do you want to make a plan based on the assumption that you can still buy perishables to fill in holes in your recipes? We recommend at least allowing for frozen foods but it's a personal decision. Once you have decided which types of foods you want in your 3 month plan, you'll be able to filter your recipes to fit that criteria. While it's always good to have some shelf stable recipes, planning strictly shelf stable meals is a hard place to start for beginners.

HOW WILL I PLAN WHAT TO BUY FOR MY SUPPLY?

Some people find that just buying the foods they regularly use in bulk quantities fits their 3 month plan goals. Some people like to plan their meals on our 3 month supply worksheets {found on pages 79-80} with good old fashioned pens and pencils.

HOW MUCH MONEY CAN I AFFORD TO BUDGET?

The end goal with your 3 month supply is to use foods daily from your pantry, and constantly replace them with your regular grocery shopping. However, to get your supply kick-started you may need to budget a certain amount of money to get things going. Figure out what you can spare until you have a supply built up and think of it as an investment.

HOW WILL I SHOP FOR MY 3 MONTH SUPPLY?

When you have determined WHAT you need to buy, develop a plan to purchase. You may decide buying one extra each time works for you, or you might get into coupon and sale shopping and buy things only when on sale. Whatever fits your style, having a game plan in place will surely help. We love the service Deals to Meals to help with this.

3 Month Supply Planning

The 3 Month Supply worksheets allow you to plan meals for three months and tally up the quantity of items you need to purchase. You decide how many different meals you want to plan and then adjust the math to equal 90 days worth of meals. There are two sheets, the Menu Plan Sheet and the Inventory Sheet.

MENU PLAN SHEET:

1. Photocopy as many Menu Plan pages as you need depending on how much variety your family likes. Plan anywhere from 10-90 days of menus. If you plan only 10 days you will multiply your ingredients needed by 9 to get 90 days
2. Input the ingredients you will need for each meal for the number of days you have printed

INVENTORY SHEET:

1. Input each ingredient you need from your menus in the Ingredient List on your Inventory Sheet. Go through each day and tally the number quantity of each ingredient you will need
2. Fill out the # needed for 3 months column on the Inventory Sheet from your tallies
3. Use the Inventory Sheet to:
   - track prices
   - keep track of your food on hand
   - tell you how many of each item you still need to purchase

Menu Plan:

Breakfast

Ingredient	Size	Quantity

Lunch

Ingredient	Size	Quantity

Dinner

Ingredient	Size	Quantity

Snacks

Ingredient	Size	Quantity

Menu Plan:

Breakfast

Ingredient	Size	Quantity

Lunch

Ingredient	Size	Quantity

Dinner

Ingredient	Size	Quantity

Snacks

Ingredient	Size	Quantity

Inventory Sheet

Ingredient	Store	Brand	Price	Size	$/size	# For 3 months	Cost for 3 month supply	Have on hand	Need to buy

BABYSTEP 4: LONG TERM PLAN

INTRODUCTION:

★ Understanding Long Term Food Storage
- Understand the basic recommended long-term foods and how they are used to help you determine what to store.
- Talk to experts in the food storage industry by going to preparedness store classes or to local church seminars.
- Assess the foods your family typically eats and how they fit into a long term plan.

★ Determining What to Purchase
- Determine the quantities you will need by using a Long Term Food Storage Calculator {found on pages 84-85}
- Start small. Work on a full 3 month supply, then move onto 6 months, then a full year.
- Follow the BabySteps Checklists {starting on page 8} to help spread out your purchases over time.

★ Learning to Use Long Term Food Storage
- Use food storage recipe books and websites for help with learning how to use your long term food storage
- Help your family gradually become accustomed to eating your Long Term Food Storage. This will ease the transition in case of an emergency.
- Talk to your friends and family members about how they use their food storage.

★ Adapt to Fit Your Family's Needs
- If you have an allergy, replace that item with something from the same category.
- If you are interested in storing healthier options, substitute with a suitable replacement.
- If there is an item you or your family don't care for, don't store it.

INSIDE THIS SECTION:

Food Storage Myths
Long Term Storage Planning
Long Term Storage Calculator
Food Storage Shelf Life
All About Oxygen Absorbers
Food Storage and Allergies
Healthy Food Storage

Food Storage Myths

YOU HAVE TO STICK TO FOOD STORAGE CALCULATORS:

Don't be afraid to replace certain foods with foods you use more often. The typical calculator may tell you to store way more, or less, of a certain ingredient than you would ever use. Replace items that you don't use with items you would use.

YOU CAN ONLY MAKE SHELF-STABLE MEALS:

While shelf stable recipes can be useful and are good to know about in case of a severe emergency situation, they are not the be all/end all of food storage. The idea is that you will be learning to cook with your food storage and constantly rotating it. It's okay to mix and match "food storage" items with "non-food storage" items.

FOOD STORAGE IS ONLY FOR PEOPLE WITH LARGE HOMES:

Total lie! Read Small Spaces Storage Solutions {found on pages 61-65} for ideas on how to start no matter how tiny you think your house might be.

YOU SHOULD BUY ALL YOUR FOOD STORAGE AT ONCE:

Not! Let's be honest, unless you have tons of cash lying around, this isn't going to happen. Start small. Commit yourself to buying food little by little. Decide you will gather small amounts of a variety of long term food storage items. Once you discover which items you use most often, re-adjust and keep on buying when you can.

FOOD STORAGE IS ONLY FOR HEALTH NUTS WHO COOK WEIRD MEALS:

False. You can incorporate food storage items into foods your family typically eats all the time. Remember, once ground, wheat is just flour. Powdered milk is milk you can use in all your recipes that call for milk.

ONLY PEOPLE WHO BAKE DESSERTS CAN ACTUALLY USE THEIR FOOD STORAGE:

Everyday food storage means using your food storage in meals you would typically make. It's surprising how you can adapt and start using your food storage even if you don't cook the standard meals or desserts "everyone" else seems to be making.

FOOD STORAGE WILL ONLY BE USEFUL IN A MAJOR NATURAL DISASTER:

While this is the reason a lot of people think you should get into food storage, it is one of the very last reasons that people end up using food storage. While it's good to eventually make plans for how to survive without things like gas and electricity, there is no need to let that get in the way of you starting to use and rotate through your food storage today!

Long Term Storage Planning

The Long Term Food Storage Calculator can help serve as a guide for your family's storage needs, as an inventory sheet of what you have stored, and what you still need to purchase.

TO USE THE CALCULATOR SHEET:

1. Go to the Long Term Storage Calculator {found on pages 84-85}.
2. Multiply the number of adults and children over 7 in your family times the standard per adult for each ingredient, and fill in the "needed for adults" column.
3. Multiply the number of children under 7 in your family by the standard per child for each ingredient, and fill in the "needed for children" column.
4. Add the "needed for adults" column and the "needed for children" column and put that sum in the "total to store" column.
5. Fill out the "cost/unit" column with the prices of each ingredient.
6. Multiply the "total to store" column by the "cost/unit" column for your "total cost" column.
7. Inventory what you have on hand and put it in the "have stored" column.
8. Subtract the "have stored" column from the "total to store" column to get how much you "need to purchase" column.

CALCULATOR ALTERATIONS:

- For food groups such as grains, legumes and sugars feel free to swap out types of foods pound for pound. For example, if there is a grain like quinoa that you would rather store, subtract it out of the same amount of a different, less preferred grain in the calculator.
- If you have young children you may consider storing more dry milk. The 16 lbs of dry milk found on the calculator will only give you 1 cup of milk per day.
- The calculator is based on traditional, life-sustaining foods with long shelf lives. Because of this, there are no recommendations for fruits, vegetables, and meats. You may choose to supplement your storage with these items (and we highly recommend it).

Long Term Storage Calculator

Family Name:	Per Adult	Per Kid	Need for Adults	Need for Kids	Total	Unit	Cost /Unit	Total Cost	Have	Need
GRAINS										
Wheat	200	100				lbs				
Flour	25	12				lbs				
Corn Meal	25	12				lbs				
Oats	50	25				lbs				
Rice	40	20				lbs				
Barley	10	5				lbs				
Pasta	50	25				lbs				
Total Grains	400	200				lbs				
FATS AND OILS										
Shortening	4	2				lbs				
Vegetable Oil	2	1				gal				
Mayonnaise	2	1				qts				
Salad Dressing	1	1				qts				
Peanut Butter	4	2				lbs				
LEGUMES										
Beans, dry	50	25				lbs				
Split Peas	5	2.5				lbs				
Lentils	5	2.5				lbs				
Dry Soup Mix	2	0.5				lbs				
Total Legumes	62	31				lbs				

Family Name:	Per Adult	Per Kid	Need for Adults	Need for Kids	Total	Unit	Cost /Unit	Total Cost	Have	Need
SUGARS										
Honey	3	1				lbs				
Sugar	40	20				lbs				
Brown Sugar	3	1				lbs				
Molasses	1	1				lbs				
Corn Syrup	3	1				lbs				
Jams	3	1				lbs				
Drink Mix	6	3				lbs				
Flavored Gelatin	1	1				lbs				
Total Sugars	60	29				lbs				
MILK										
Dry Milk*	16	8				lbs				
COOKING ESSENTIALS										
Powdered Eggs	4	2				lbs				
Baking Powder	1	1				lbs				
Baking Soda	1	1				lbs				
Yeast	1	0.5				lbs				
Salt	8	4				lbs				
Vinegar	0.5	0.5				gal				

If you have young children you may consider storing more dry milk. 16 lbs of dry milk will only give you 1 cup of milk per day.

Food Storage Shelf Life Chart

Grains		
Product	**Optimum Shelf Life**	**Opened Shelf Life**
Whole Wheat Flour	5 years	2 years
White Flour	5 years	2 years
Hard White Winter Wheat	30 years	30 years
6 Grain Pancake Mix	8 years	1 year
Spaghetti	8 years	2 years
Egg Noodle Pasta	8 years	2 years
Quick Oats	8 years	1 year
White Rice	30 years	30 years
Instant White Rice	30 years	30 years
Pearled Barley	8 years	18 months
Cornmeal	5 years	1 year
9 Grain Cracked Cereal	5 years	1 year
Elbow Macaroni	8 years	2 years
Germade	5 years	18 months

Vegetables		
Product	**Optimum Shelf Life**	**Opened Shelf Life**
Bell Peppers	8 years	2 years
Split Green Peas	8 years	2 years
Mushroom Pieces (Freeze-Dried)	25 years	2 years
Potato Chunks (Freeze-Dried)	25 years	2 years
Sweet Corn (Freeze-Dried)	25 years	2 years
Tomato Powder	8 years	1 year
Green Peas (Freeze-Dried)	25 years	2 years
Cauliflower (Freeze-Dried)	25 years	2 years
Carrot Dices	8 years	2 years
Broccoli (Freeze-Dried)	25 years	2 years
Celery (Freeze-Dried)	25 years	2 years
Celery	25 years	2 years
Spinach (Freeze-Dried)	25 years	2 years
Onions (Freeze-Dried)	25 years	2 years

Fruits		
Product	**Optimum Shelf Life**	**Opened Shelf Life**
Apple Chips	7 years	1 year
Peach Slices (Freeze-Dried)	25 years	1 year
Raspberries (Freeze-Dried)	25 years	1 year
Strawberries (Freeze-Dried)	25 years	1 year
Blueberries (Freeze-Dried)	25 years	1 year

Food Storage Made Easy

Blackberries (Freeze-Dried)	25 years	1 year
Applesauce	7 years	6 months (refrigerated)
Apple Slices	30 years	30 years
Banana Chips	7 years	1 year
Blackberries	25 years	1 year

Dairy		
Product	**Optimum Shelf Life**	**Opened Shelf Life**
Chocolate Drink Mix	25 years	1-2 years
Cheese Powder	15 years	1-2 years
Non-Fat Powdered Milk	25 years	1-2 years

Meats and Beans		
Product	**Optimum Shelf Life**	**Opened Shelf Life**
Black Beans	30 years	5 years
Small Red Beans	30 years	5 years
Whole Eggs	5 years	6 months
Taco TVP	10 years	1 year
Sausage TVP	10 years	1 year
Pinto Beans	30 years	5 years
Chicken TVP	10 years	1 year
Beef TVP	10 years	1 year
Ham TVP	10 years	1 year
Kidney Beans	30 years	5 years
Lima Beans	30 years	5 years
Lentils	30 years	5 years
Bacon TVP	10 years	1 year

Basics		
Product	**Optimum Shelf Life**	**Opened Shelf Life**
Orange Drink	3 years	6 months to 1 year
Iodized Salt	30 years	2 years
Chicken Bouillon	5 years	2 years
Peach Drink	3 years	6 months to 1 year
White Sugar	30 years	2 years
Powdered Sugar	30 years	12 to 18 months
Baking Soda	30 years	2 years
Apple Drink	3 years	6 months to 1 year
Baking Powder	30 years	2 years
Beef Bouillon	5 years	2 years
Brown Sugar	10 years	1 year

* Best storage conditions are a cool dry environment under 70 degrees.

* Optimum shelf life is the shelf life with the best taste and nutritional value.

* Life sustaining shelf lives can be much longer than the optimum shelf life.

* This chart was modified from a list found at Thrive Life

All About Oxygen Absorbers

Oxygen absorbers help preserve food quality. They are used when dry foods are packaged in sealed containers.

Oxygen absorbers are small packets that contain an iron powder. The packets are made of a material that allows oxygen and moisture to enter but does not allow the iron powder to leak out.

Products should be low in moisture and oil content. If the moisture content is not low enough (about 10 percent or less), storing products in reduced oxygen packaging may result in botulism poisoning. Make sure you are only storing foods that are dry enough.

TYPES OF CONTAINERS TO BE USED WITH OXYGEN ABSORBERS:

Oxygen absorbers should be used with containers that provide an effective barrier against moisture and oxygen. The following containers work well:

- Metal cans with seamed lids.
- Foil/mylar pouches.
- PETE plastic bottles with airtight, screw-on lids.
- Glass canning jars with metal lids that have gaskets.

Oxygen absorbers are not an effective treatment method for plastic buckets, milk bottles, or other types of plastic bottles not identified as PETE or PET under the recycle symbol.

PROPER WAY TO USE OXYGEN ABSORBERS:

Here are step-by-step instructions on using oxygen absorbers:

1. Cut open the top of the bag of absorbers. Do not open the individual absorber packets.

2. Remove the number of absorbers from the bag that you will use in the next 20 to 30 minutes, and spread them out on a tray. Remove additional groups of absorbers from the supply as you need them during the packaging process, but do not open and close the bag repeatedly to get only a few absorbers at a time.

3. Reseal the remaining supply of absorbers by one of the following methods. Do not store absorbers in ziplock bags.
   - Seal the bag of absorbers with a clamp
   - Seal the bag of absorbers with an impulse heat sealer.
   - For longer storage when an impulse sealer is not available, remove the absorbers from the bag and place them into a glass canning jar that has a metal lid with a gasket. A one-pint jar (500 ml) will hold 25 absorbers.

4. Place one absorber into each container of food as it is packaged.

Food Storage Made Easy

Food Storage and Allergies

While food storage calculators are nice to have, they can feel irrelevant if you have a food allergy or other dietary limitations. Planning a food storage when you or a family member has an allergy can feel overwhelming and tricky. Here are some tips to help you adapt and make a plan for your food storage.

ADAPTING TO THE ALLERGY:

When you find out you have an allergy to a certain type of food, through trial and error you will figure out how you might choose to adapt.

The most common allergy you might need to adapt to is a gluten allergy. Here are two options you might have to navigate and decide what is best for you:

1. Go forward living without the types of foods that contain gluten, make other choices and stock accordingly. For example, you could choose to eat more rice, corn, quinoa, and a variety of other grains and make meals that these grains are typically found in. In other words, say goodbye to breads etc.

2. Go forward trying to modify recipes to mimic some of your favorite items that typically contain gluten. For example, you may find a way to make pizza dough, breads, pancakes and other pastries using substitutions that are gluten-free.

Before deciding on a course of action, determine how you will choose to live your regular daily life. Once you have figured out what your new lifestyle will be, make a plan keeping that in mind.

MAKING THE PLAN:

Use the food storage calculator and adapt to your needs. Use that list as a starting point, and then start doing replacements. So, for example, if you can't eat gluten, substitute pound for pound other grains in place of wheat.

If you decide to use recipes that call for ingredients that you need to make your bread, pancakes, etc. gluten-free, make sure you store the necessary ingredients for that.

So here is a break down step-by-step:
1. Determine what foods you eat
2. Replace foods you can't eat on a standard calculator
3. Add foods you need to make your new diet come together to the standard calculator

Healthy Food Storage

There is not a one size fits all recommendation for what to put in your food storage. If your family is concerned with natural foods and medicines, here are some recommendations and ideas.

BASIC GUIDELINES:

- Eat foods in their wholesome natural state
- Study nutrition and herbs
- Avoid forming toxic habits
- When soaked and sprouted, wheat is the staff of life
- Eat foods in their season

HEALTHY OPTIONS CALCULATOR:

300 lbs Organic Wheat
155 lbs Other Grains
50 lbs Nuts
50 lbs Seeds
75 lbs Organic Beans
60 lbs Raw Honey
20 lbs Oil (coconut oil, olive oil, wheat germ oil)
10 lbs Salt (real salt)
60 lbs Sprout Mix
5 lbs Seed Sprout mix
Garden Seeds (non hybrid)
Spices

HERBS FOR MEDICINE:

Here are some benefits to storing herbs and oils for medicine:

Long shelf life: Some remedies have up to a 7 year shelf life or longer if stored properly.

Versatile: With natural medicines, most of the time you can use the same remedy to both prevent and treat a problem. Additionally, the same natural remedies that an adult takes, a child can take, too. Most herbs have multiple applications (i.e. you can use the same herb to treat the flu and a cold).

You can make them yourself: With the exception of essential oils, you can make all your remedies yourself and it's pretty easy, too.

Super cheap: Even if you don't make them yourself, most of the time they are the same price, if not cheaper, than their conventional counterparts.

BABYSTEP 5: GRAINS

INTRODUCTION:

★ Grains are used to create the foundation of your long-term food storage and a wide variety of foods.

★ It is recommended that half your daily grain intake be whole grains due to the high nutritional value and protein levels (examples: whole wheat, oats, brown rice, etc).

★ Accumulate recipes that include grains. Using your grains regularly will help you rotate through them and get your family used to eating and digesting them.

★ Even though you can store other grains, wheat is the most basic and most versatile grain. It's "the staff of life".

★ Examples of some of the more typical grains are: wheat, oats, cornmeal, popcorn, barley, rice, quinoa.

★ Grinding grains tends to be a major hang up for most people. Learn why not to be intimidated by grain mills by reading All About Grain Mills {found on pages 97-98}.

★ Food Storage Made Easy recommends the WonderMill or NutriMill when the time is right for your family to invest in a grain mill.

★ Determine the quantities of each food item you will need to store. For more information see Long Term Food Storage Planning {found on page 83}.

INSIDE THIS SECTION:

All About Wheat
All About Oats
All About Rice
All About Cornmeal/Popcorn
All About Barley
All About Grain Mills
Bread-Making FAQ
Using Wheat Without A Wheat Grinder

All About Wheat

Hard or soft: Hard wheat varieties have higher gluten levels (protein) and are better for making breads. Soft varieties have lower protein and nutrients but are better for pastries, pastas, and breakfast cereals.

Red or white: Red wheat tends to have a stronger wheat flavor than white wheat. Most red wheat varieties are hard, and most white wheat varieties are soft, but you can find soft red and hard white if you really prefer one over the other. Hard white wheat is our favorite all-purpose wheat to store and is what we use in our favorite bread recipe.

Spring or winter: Winter red wheat tends to have a slightly higher protein content and is a bit harder than spring red wheat. Winter red is better for baking bread than spring. There is not a significant difference in winter or spring varieties of white wheat.

Remember, don't confuse fresh ground whole grain white wheat flour with store-bought white flour. Whole white wheat is slightly lighter in color than red wheat, but has almost the same nutritional value. Store- bought white flour has had all the nutrients stripped from it in the refining process and therefore adds little nutritional value to recipes.

BENEFITS OF WHEAT:

- Wheat can be stored for over 30 years if kept in a cool, dry place
- Whole wheat is a whole grain and it retains all of the vitamins, minerals, and fiber
- There are no preservatives or additives in wheat you grind yourself
- You can sprout wheat and use it in smoothies, salads, soups, etc.
- You can use wheat to extend your meat

STORAGE:

- If unopened, the optimum shelf life of wheat is around 12 years. It is still edible for 30 years or even longer than that, but won't necessarily keep the same flavor or nutrient levels and will lose it's ability to sprout. If opened, it will stay good for about 3 years.
- Once ground into flour, wheat will go rancid fairly quickly unless stored in the freezer.
- Add oxygen absorbers, bay leaves, or dry ice to help keep critters out of your wheat and to extend shelf life.

ROTATION:

You should constantly be rotating your wheat in your food storage. One method to do this is to have several buckets of wheat well-sealed with oxygen absorbers. Open one bucket at a time and "work" out of that bucket. Bring up a Tupperware container full of wheat every few weeks so that it is in your kitchen where you will be able to access it easily and use it on a regular basis. When that "working bucket" is empty you will know you need to buy a new bucket and it moves to the end of your rotation.

All About Oats

TYPES OF OATS:

For long term food storage purposes you should consider storing one the following varieties of oats (and not instant oats or oatmeal):

Steel Cut Oats: This variety is often sold in bulk or in #10 cans at emergency preparedness stores. These are oat groats which have been cut into chunks with steel blades. They're not rolled and look like coarse bits of grain.

Rolled Oats: This variety is your typical grocery store variety. Rolled oats are made by steaming oat groats and then rolling them flat. They take longer to cook than quick-cooking oats, but retain more flavor and nutrition.

Quick-Cooking Rolled Oats: Quick-cooking rolled oats are not to be confused with "instant oatmeal" where you just add water and microwave. They are simply rolled oats that have been rolled a little bit flatter to reduce the cooking time.

Oat Groats: Oat groats are the grains that are used to make steel-cut, rolled and quick oats. They look kind of like wheat and can be crushed with a grain flaker, or can be ground in a grain mill to make flour. Storing oat groats may not be as convenient as storing the other options.

BENEFITS OF OATS:

Oats are considered a "whole grain" because both rolled and cut oats retain their bran and their germ. Whole grains are recommended to be at least 50% of your daily grain intake due to their benefit to cardiovascular health, weight management, and other nutritional advantages.

You can also use oats with minimal cooking which is an advantage in situations where fuel conservation is important.

USES OF OATS:

Oats are not just for oatmeal. Oats can be used in the following foods:
• Cookies
• Granola bars
• Topping for fruit desserts
• Meat fillers
• Pancakes
• To make sprouts

All About Rice

TYPES OF RICE:

There are over 40,000 different varieties of rice, but people usually store only the most common ones. It is generally recommended you store the type that your family prefers to eat, but there are some shelf life considerations with that.

Brown Rice: Brown rice is considered a whole grain. The outer husk is removed but the bran and germ remain intact. This provides a lot of fiber and allows the rice to retain its nutrients. There are many colors, shapes, and sizes of brown rice including long, medium, and short grains, basmati, red, purple, black and many more.

White Rice: White rice is any variety of rice that has had the bran and germ removed and been completely milled and polished. Normally vitamins and minerals are added back in to improve the nutrient content of the food. White rice has a long shelf life so it is great for long term food storage.

INSTANT VS NON-INSTANT RICE:

Instant rice is simply rice that has been fully cooked and then dried before packaging. This allows it to have a much shorter cook time since it doesn't have to be fully cooked again. Typically instant rice is more expensive than regular rice. You can buy instant brown or white rice.

SHELF LIFE OF RICE:

White rice has a shelf life of up to 30 years if it is stored in a cool dry place.
Brown rice from the store typically only lasts about 6-8 months due to the oil content in it. Commercially-packaged instant brown rice designed for longer term storage often has a longer shelf life.

USES OF RICE:

Most people know how to cook traditional meals with rice. It is great as a filler in soups and casseroles, as a side dish for meat/chicken dishes with sauces, spiced up for a delicious Mexican side dish, or as a staple of Chinese food cooking.

HOW TO COOK RICE:

Many people cook rice in rice cookers. You can also cook rice in a pot on a stovetop, or a camping stove. Another great tool to use is a pressure cooker. One unexpected way to cook rice should you be without power is a Sun Oven.

All About Cornmeal/Popcorn

TYPES OF CORNMEAL:

Steel ground: The most common type of cornmeal, it has the husk and germ almost all removed. Because of this, steel ground cornmeal has less flavor and nutrients but does have a very long shelf life. This is the type you will typically find at the grocery store.

Stone ground: This type of cornmeal retains more of the husk and germ but because of this it is more perishable than steel ground.

Cornmeal can be found in white, yellow, red, and blue. Yellow and white are most common.

TYPES OF CORN:

The basic types of dried corn used for food storage are: flint, dent, and popcorn. All can be used fairly interchangeably but flint is a little better for cornmeal, dent is better for corn masa, and popcorn is the most versatile since it can be popped for a snack or ground into meal or flour. Corn can be found in white, yellow, red, and blue. Yellow corn is often recommended over white, since white corn doesn't contain carotene (which converts into vitamin A). Yellow dent corn is very common at food storage stores, but popcorn can easily be found at grocery stores.

SHELF LIFE OF CORNMEAL/CORN:

Cornmeal: Between 6 and 18 months. Store in a cool dry place to help prolong this.
Corn: 8 years or more if stored in a sealed airtight container with an oxygen absorber.

USES OF CORNMEAL/CORN:

Dried corn can be used as a vegetable in stews, popped into popcorn, or ground into flour or cornmeal. Corn flour is most commonly used to make corn masa which is a dough used to make tortillas. Cornmeal (fresh ground or store bought) can be used to make delicious cornbread or pancakes. It can also be made into hominy or grits.

RECOMMENDATIONS:

It is recommended you purchase a small amount of cornmeal and try some food storage recipes out and see if your family likes eating those foods. If it turns out to be something you really like, then you should store a lot of popcorn and grind it into fresh cornmeal which helps with flavor and gives you more nutrients. If you don't have a wheat grinder available to you, try to buy cornmeal in good sealed containers such as #10 cans to help prolong the shelf life.

All About Barley

WHAT IS BARLEY:

Barley is a grain with short, stubby kernels and a hull that is difficult to remove. It is often used in soups or stews as a filler and to add some extra chewiness. It is a good source of fiber and niacin, and is also low in fat with no saturated fat or cholesterol.

TYPES OF BARLEY:

There are two types of barley, a refined (white) variety and a "whole grain" variety.

Pearl Barley: The most common type of barley is the white, highly processed "pearl" barley that has had most of its bran and germ removed along with its hull. It is the least nutritious form of barley but has a fairly long shelf life.

Pot Barley: The second variety is called "pot" or "hulled" barley and it has been subjected to the same milling process as pearled, but with fewer trips through the polisher. Because of this, it retains more of the nutritious germ and bran.

STORING BARLEY:

Since pearl barley is so highly processed (similar to white rice) it has a much longer shelf life than pot barley. If you enjoy barley and plan to store a fair amount of it, then definitely store mostly pearl barley. However, if you are going to be using it a lot and rotating through it on a regular basis it would be beneficial to store at least some of it in the pot barley variety in order to have the benefit of additional nutrients.

BUYING BARLEY:

You can occasionally find bags of pearl barley at the grocery store near the beans and rice. You can also purchase boxes of Quaker Quick Barley which is found in the same section and typically easier to find than the bags. If you can't find it at your grocery store, or you want to buy it in bulk, your best option is to purchase online.

USING BARLEY:

You can use barley in all sorts of stews the way you would use rice or noodles. You may want to adjust cooking times and liquid if you aren't using pearl or quick barley. The barley will add a little bit of flavor, texture, and nutrients. You can also grind barley in your grain mill and use it to make multi-grain flours to be used in muffins, pancakes, and other baked goods.

All About Grain Mills

Grain mills are one of the most useful appliances to have when using and rotating your food storage. A lot of people think grain mills, are only for wheat, however they can be used with all sorts of grains, legumes, and more.

MANUAL GRAIN MILLS:

Pros:
- Basic models are inexpensive however good ones are similar in cost to electric mills
- Can be used with no power source so they are great for emergency situations
- Many models are very small thus requiring little storage space
- Able to grind items such as oily seeds, nuts, herbs, and coffee that would normally ruin an electric mill

Cons:
- SLOW to grind (can take 5-6 minutes to grind one cup of flour)
- Except for the higher-end models, you cannot grind grain into a fine flour
- Some models are inconvenient (messy and hard to fit a large bowl underneath)

KITCHENAID ATTACHMENTS:

Pros:
- Less expensive than an electric grinder
- Small to store
- Convenient to use the grinder attachment and then mix bread dough in the same machine

Cons:
- We have heard from multiple sources that these units will break your KitchenAid mixer
- Must have a generator or battery pack to use with no electricity
- Not as fast at grinding as electric grinders

ELECTRIC GRAIN MILLS:

Pros:
- Grinds VERY quickly thus making it easy to use in your everyday cooking
- Easy to select how coarse or fine to grind your grains
- Large capacity for grinding a lot of grains/legumes at a time

Cons:
- Fairly expensive, even for the lower-end models
- Must have a generator or battery pack to use with no electricity
- Large appliance to store in your kitchen
- Not able to grind oily seeds, nuts, or herbs

Manual Grain Mills:
- Low: $20-30 models will not grind flour, only coarse corn meal, etc.
- Medium: $75-$225 is a good price range. Back to Basics Grain Mill can be found for around $70. It can grind fine enough for bread flour but not for very fine cake flour. The Wonder Junior Deluxe is more expensive is heavy duty, can grind flours of all consistencies, can be used for nut butters, and grinds quicker than cheaper options. The Family Grain Mill is a mid-range manual mill, but has the option to include a motorized base. You can also attach it to a Bosch if you don't want to purchase the base.
- High: Up to $400 for the Country Living Grain Mill. It is quicker than other manual grinders and is able to grind a fine cake flour (can also add a small motor to it to make it electric).

KitchenAid Attachments:
- $80-120, some may be used on any stand mixer.

Electric Grain Mills:
- Low: Under $200 for grinders such as the Blendtec Grain Mill. This model is very noisy and cannot grind at a very coarse setting.
- Medium: $200-$300 can get you a great grinder. The two most popular electric grinders are the WonderMill and the NutriMill.
- High: You can purchase the Country Living Manual Grain Mill for $400 and add a small motor to it to function as an electric mill.

WHEAT GRINDER RECOMMENDATIONS:

Emergency-Only Usage:
If you are planning to use your food storage and wheat grinder only if an emergency situation arises, it is not worth the expense and hassle of buying and storing an electric grinder. At a minimum you should get the Back to Basics Grain Mill which will enable you to at least bake bread. However, the Wonder Junior Deluxe will do everything an electric grinder does and grind quicker and better than the Back to Basics Grain Mill. The Family Grain Mill might be a good option as well since you could have both the manual and electric functions.

Everyday Usage:
If you plan to "store what you eat and eat what you store" you should consider an Electric Grain Mill. If you are worried about what to do without power, you can pick up an additional hand grinder at a later time, or work on alternate power sources. Due to the functionality and ease of use, an electric mill is the best option for frequent usage. It also helps you rotate your grains more frequently.

Bread-Making FAQ

In our recipe appendix we share our favorite bread recipe (entitled "Best Whole Wheat Bread Recipe"). We have been asked quite a few questions about making bread over the years so we put together this FAQ to help give you a little more confidence as you embark on this part of your food storage journey.

DO YOU HAVE TO USE A STAND MIXER TO MAKE THIS BREAD?

Definitely not. Since you never know the reason you may be living off of your food storage, it's a good idea to make sure you can prepare food without using electricity. We have experimented with making this recipe using no electric kitchen tools. We ground the wheat in a manual wheat grinder, kneaded it by hand, and cooked it in an All-American Sun Oven. Kneading by hand takes some time and a little bit of hard work but it definitely still turns out great without using a Bosch or KitchenAid.

DO YOU HAVE A RECIPE THAT IS NOT SO LARGE?

This recipe is actually very easy to cut in half and still have good results. If you still end up with too much dough consider making bread plus rolls to freeze for later or a pizza crust to use for dinner. If you want a recipe specifically designed to be a one loaf recipe, try the Honey Whole Wheat Bread recipe {found on page 158}. It's a great recipe but doesn't use 100% whole wheat.

DO YOU HAVE TO USE VITAL WHEAT GLUTEN?

One of our favorite things about our favorite bread recipe is the texture. We feel that vital wheat gluten and the "sponging" process are the keys to this as we have not had any other recipes turn out as well without using other additives. If you don't want to use vital wheat gluten you can try using Wheat Protein Isolate (found at Honeyville Grain). You should be able to get similar results using about 1/3 or 1/2 as much product.

There are several other things that can be used as dough enhancers but we recommend finding a recipe that uses them specifically instead of trying to sub them into this recipe in place of the gluten.

CAN THIS RECIPE BE FROZEN FOR USE LATER?

Yes it can. Freezing this dough works similar to frozen Rhodes Rolls. You will need to remove the loaves or rolls from the freezer with enough time to let them thaw and rise. If you use the dough for pizza crust you can either roll it out after it thaws, or freeze it on your pizza pan already rolled out.

HOW DO YOU USE THIS DOUGH FOR PIZZA?

There are two methods you can use to make a pizza dough. First make a half recipe, and then split that into 3 equal parts. You can use two for bread and the third for pizza. Roll it out and use it on a regular pizza pan or pizza stone. Let rise for 30-60 minutes depending on how thick you'd like your crust. Spray your pan with pam spray if you're not using a stone. Add sauce, cheese, and other toppings and cook for about 15 minutes at 425 or until the dough is firm and cheese is fully melted and lightly browned. If you like crunchy crust, you can take the pizza and put it directly on the rack for the last 3-4 minutes. Whole wheat pizza takes a little longer to cook than pizza made with white flour, but it tastes great and is healthier and more filling.

If you like a deeper dish pizza you can follow these directions instead. To make one large pizza crust, use about a quarter batch of dough (or make a half batch and use the extra for bread or rolls). Use a cookie sheet that has sides on it. This makes a large pizza with a thick crust. Melt about 1/2 cup of butter in the pizza pan in the oven. Pull it out and set your dough on it. Spread the dough out with your hands all the way to the edges flipping it over a few times to get it covered in butter. Let it rise a little while you pull out all your toppings. Don't let it rise for very long as this is already quite a thick crust. The consistency turns out thick and chewy almost like breadsticks. Bake at 425 for 10-15 minutes or until everything is golden brown and the dough is firm.

CAN I SUBSTITUTE AGAVE FOR THE HONEY/SUGAR?

While we have not personally tried this, we have a friend who always makes bread with Agave. We would recommend following the normal recommendations for Agave and use slightly less than the called for amount of honey.

DO YOU HAVE TO GREASE YOUR PANS BEFORE PUTTING THE DOUGH IN?

Yes definitely. It will make it much easier to get the cooked loaves out when they are finished cooking.

HOW CAN I KEEP MY CRUST FROM GETTING TOO DARK?

Check on your bread after about 10-15 minutes. If it looks like it is getting dark but not quite cooked yet, put a layer of tinfoil over the top. It will give you a perfect light brown crust.

WHAT TYPE OF WHEAT SHOULD I USE FOR THIS RECIPE?

Our favorite is hard white wheat as it seems to have less of a "wheaty" flavor. However if you like that strong wheat flavor hard red wheat will work too.

WHAT IS THE BENEFIT OF USING FRESH WHEAT FLOUR VERSUS ALL-PURPOSE FLOUR?

There are two big benefits to having whole wheat in your food storage. First is the shelf life. Wheat will store almost indefinitely making it a great item to keep on hand without having to worry as much about rotation. Second, the health benefits of using whole grains are immense. All-purpose flour has been stripped of most of the nutrients in order to give it a longer shelf life in it's ground state.

DO YOU HAVE TO USE FRESH GROUND WHEAT EVERY TIME?

When you grind your wheat it will lose a lot of the nutrients after 24 hours. It will also go rancid within a few weeks. If you store the wheat in your freezer it will keep it from going rancid but the nutrients will still be less than if fresh-ground. Ideally you would grind it before making each batch, but a lot of times it's easier to grind a big batch of wheat and store it in the freezer.

WHAT KIND OF YEAST DO YOU USE?

We use SAF instant yeast. When you use instant yeast, you don't have to "proof" it. Proofing yeast is when you add it to hot water and wait until it activates before combining it with other ingredients. We like using SAF instant yeast because you can throw it into the recipe and not have any worries.

WHAT SHOULD THE CONSISTENCY OF THE DOUGH FEEL LIKE?

Your dough should feel a little on the sticky side. If you over-flour, or add flour after you have done the kneading, you will get a crumbly bread. If your dough is too sticky to handle, spray it with Pam and spray the counter with Pam. That will make your dough more workable and fluffy.

Using Wheat Without a Grinder

1. THERMOS WHEAT

Bring 1 c. of wheat kernels, 2 c. water, and 1 t. salt to a boil in a medium saucepan. Pour into a heated stainless steel or glass-lined thermos bottle. Secure cap. Place bottle on side and lest sit overnight. In the morning, pour off any water, add butter and honey, and serve hot.

2. WHEAT BERRIES

Add some of your plain dry wheat kernels to a pot of water. Bring it to a boil and cook for a few minutes. Let simmer for about 45 minutes. Drain the wheat berries and stick them in a tupperware in the fridge. These are delicious to add to yogurt or to use to replace some meat in recipes. You can also use it in place of brown rice.

3. POPPED WHEAT

Take 1 cup of cooked wheat berries (see above) and add to a frying pan or pot with two tablespoons of oil in it. Cover with a lid and cook over a hot stove shaking the pan while it cooks. After about 4-5 minutes the kernels will be nice and toasted. Put the popped wheat on a paper towel to absorb the extra oil, and sprinkle with your choice of seasonings. These are delicious on salads as a topping, mixed with trail mix, as toppings for desserts, or just as a healthy snack.

4. WHEAT GRASS

Most people have heard how healthy wheat grass is for you, but most people don't know that you can make your own wheat grass at home for free with just a little bit of your food storage wheat. You can snip bits off and add them to some delicious fruit smoothies, or if you have a juicer you can use them in other healthy juice drinks.

5. CRACKED WHEAT

You can crack wheat in a blender or a coffee grinder. To do it in a blender you simply put in about 1/4-1/3 cups of wheat and pulse it until it looks like little cracked kernels. These kernels will cook much faster than regular wheat, and cook up in the same way that you cook rice on the stove. You can use cracked wheat to make hot cereal, add it into bread, or cook it and use as a meat filler.

6. WHEAT SPROUTS

Making wheat sprouts is a different method than making wheat grass. You can sprout wheat just like any other vegetable seeds, legumes, or other grains. Most people like wheat sprouts to be very small, just barely sprouted. These are delicious to throw on salads or to add into your whole wheat bread for a little extra texture and flavor.

7. BLENDER WHEAT FLOUR

If you are cooking a recipe for something like pancakes or waffles, you can easily use your whole wheat kernels, mix the whole recipe in your blender, and pour it straight from there onto a griddle or waffle-maker. Just make sure to add the liquid for your recipe into the blender, then add in your wheat kernels and blend for about 5 minutes. Then add the rest of the ingredients.

BABYSTEP 6: LEGUMES

INTRODUCTION:

★ Purchase your legumes and learn how to use them. Recommended legumes to store include: dried beans, bean soup mixes, lentils, soy beans, etc.

★ Beans, peas and lentils are the richest source of vegetable protein and are a good source of both soluble and insoluble dietary fiber.

★ Using dried beans and soaking them overnight is the best way to get the true bean flavor and a smooth texture as opposed to using canned beans. The nutrients are retained much better as well.

★ When legumes are eaten with grains, nuts, or seeds a complete protein can be formed which can suitably replace meat, fish, poultry, eggs or dairy.

★ Legumes aren't just used for soups. Some other uses are:
  • Grind into bean flour for white sauces
  • Mash up cooked beans to replace butter/oil in recipes
  • Grow into sprouts for a fresh "vegetable"

★ One easy way to start using dried beans is to use them in place of canned beans in your normal recipes.

★ Generally, legumes will keep indefinitely when stored in a cool, dry place.

★ Meats can be used to supplement or replace legumes as a protein source in your storage. Meats can be stored in the following ways:
  • Canned meats (either purchased or home-canned)
  • Dehydrated meats (beef or turkey jerky, either homemade or store-bought)
  • Freeze-dried meats (many varieties available to purchase)
  • Fresh meat from animals you raise

★ Determine the quantities of each food item you will need to store. For more information see Long Term Food Storage Planning {found on page 83}.

INSIDE THIS SECTION:

All About Dried Beans
All About Other Legumes
All About Sprouting
15 Ways To Use Sprouts
All About Meats
Using Freeze-Dried Meats

All About Dried Beans

Bean Do's:
- Store dry beans in a cool, dry place.
- Lightly rinse packaged dry beans; sort through them and remove any pebbles, seed pods, leaves or twigs.
- Soak your beans. It reduces cooking time by about one half, and saves vitamins, minerals and proteins which can be lost during prolonged heating — exceptions are lentils, split peas and black-eyed peas which may be cooked from their dry state.
- Soak beans in plenty of water. Use a 3:1 or 4:1 ratio of water to beans.
- Place presoaked beans in a pot and cover with fresh, cold water. Bring to a boil, reduce heat, partially cover and simmer them for the indicated length of time until they are soft and tender.

Bean Don'ts:
- Don't store dry beans in the refrigerator.
- Don't add salt or any product high in calcium, magnesium or acid to the soaking or cooking water or beans will not soften (products with these elements should be added to cooking water recipes only after beans have reached desired tenderness).
- Don't use microwave to cook dry beans - microwaving is fine for reheating beans that are already cooked, but dry beans need to be simmered slowly in lots of water to soften, tenderize, and plump up properly.

BENEFITS OF BEANS:

Low-Calorie Food:
When added to boiling water, bean flours thicken in only a few minutes and can become a perfect white sauce base for lots of recipes. By replacing bean flour in white sauce recipes you lower the calories dramatically because you take out the butter.

Great Protein:
Beans are an excellent source of protein, forming a complete protein when combined with rice, corn, and many other grains. Getting protein this way can help you avoid some of the fatty meat proteins.

High in Fiber:
One cup of beans provide the same amount of fiber as 3 standard doses of Metamucil. Not only do they give you the fiber, they are much more pleasant to eat and can be prepared with an endless variety of flavors.

Low in Fat:
Nearly all beans contain only 2-3% fat! You can even add oils to some recipes without going above the 10% fat level recommended by doctors.

Lower Cholesterol:
Did you know that beans can help lower your cholesterol level? Not only do they contain no cholesterol, they actually help the body get rid of what is considered bad cholesterol.

SOAKING BEANS:

Here are some methods to soak your beans

Quick Soak Method: Hot soaking helps dissolve some of the gas-causing substances. Cover beans with twice as much water as beans, bring to a boil, boil 2 minutes, remove from heat and allow to soak at least 1 hour or up to 4 hours. Discard soaking liquid.
Traditional Overnight Soak: Cover with twice as much water as beans and soak 8-18 hours in cool place, discard soaking water.
Please note: Do not salt soaking liquid. It will toughen the bean. It is not necessary to soak split peas and lentils.

COOKING LEGUMES:

1. Beans will double to triple in size during soaking and cooking. In other words, 1 cup dry beans will produce 2-3 cups of cooked beans.
2. The slower the beans are cooked the easier they are to digest. Slow cooker cooking on low for 6-10 hours is perfect.
3. If adding water to cooking beans is necessary, bring water to a boil before adding. Adding cold water to boiling beans will toughen beans and slow down the cooking process.

SOFTENING OLD BEANS:

The older the bean the tougher it is and less digestible. Following are a few tips to soften old beans.

1. Cook and freeze. The freezing moisture in the bean helps to rupture the cell wall and create a more palatable product.
2. Pressure cook. Follow manufacturer's directions for using your pressure cooker. Increase cooking time as needed to produce a desired texture.
3. Pressure-can beans. This method makes a readily usable product as well as softens beans. Follow USDA canning instructions for proper processing.

INCREASING CONSUMPTION OF BEANS:

You should eat beans about 2-3 times a week. (2½ to 3 cups per week)

1. Plan menus.
2. Puree cooked beans and add to baked goods (bread, cake, cookies, etc.). Substitute pureed beans for shortening or margarine cup for fun in recipes.
3. Prepare convenience foods such as home canned dry beans or cook and freeze for later use.
4. Add whole or mashed beans to meatloaves, soups, stews, casseroles (in small amounts to begin with, then increase as desired, and as allowed by your family's taste preferences).

All About Other Legumes

Dried beans are the most common legume. The following are other legumes to consider for use in food storage:

ALFALFA:

Alfalfa is a member of the pea family and is typically eaten as sprouts.

Uses: Alfalfa sprouts can be used to top sandwiches and burgers similar to lettuce. They are also good thrown into salads or soups. You can even set them on a plate and use as an edible garnish for a main meat dish.
Health Benefits: Alfalfa contains high levels of phytoestrogens, saponins, and antioxidants.

LENTILS:

Lentils are small, flat legumes that come in a wide variety of colors such as red, green, brown, yellow, etc.

Uses: Lentils can be flavored many different ways. You can make a sweet salad by combining them with fruits, or a savory soup or casserole. They can also be used as a meat filler or substitute to add bulk to your meals.
Health Benefits: Lentils are high in fiber and magnesium, yet low in calories and fat.

SPLIT PEAS:

Split peas are regular peas that have been dried after harvesting. After they are dried and the skins removed, they split naturally. They can usually be found in both yellow and green varieties.

Uses: The most common use for split peas is the famous split pea soup. You can also make a puree of cooked split peas as a side dish, or make "dahl", a traditional Indian dish.
Health Benefits: Split peas (like lentils) are high in fiber and low in calories and fat. They also provide a good source of 4 minerals, 2 B-vitamins, and isoflavones.

All About Sprouting

Everyone knows these typical long term food storage foods that are recommended for our storage: grains, legumes, powdered milk, etc. However, when you look at the calculators you notice a severe shortage of fresh fruits and vegetables due to their short shelf life. What most people don't realize is that your grains and legumes provide an automatic source of fresh vegetables for your storage in the form of sprouts.

COMMON TYPES OF SPROUTS:

Grains: Wheat, rice, oats, corn, barley
Legumes: Peas, lentils, soy beans, garbanzo, mung beans, dried beans, alfalfa
Nuts and Seeds: Almonds, sunflower seeds, vegetable seeds

HEALTH BENEFITS OF SPROUTS:

- Sprouting a seed enhances its already high nutritional value (i.e. Oats when sprouted contain 600% more vitamin C)
- Sprouts are high in antioxidants that prevent DNA destruction and protect from the effects of aging
- Sprouts contain concentrated amounts of phytochemicals which help protect against diseases
- Alfalfa sprouts contain saponins which:
  - Lower bad cholesterol and fat but keep the good hdl fats
  - Stimulate immune system
  - Help prevent cardiovascular disease
- Sprouts are a nutritious, low-fat filler for meats or addition to soups, etc.

HOW TO GROW SPROUTS:

1. Prepare the seeds
   - Remove broken and discolored seeds
   - Wash seeds
   - Soak overnight (if necessary)
   - Drain
2. Place seeds in sprouting container and rinse thoroughly.
3. Drain off all excess water.
4. Place in a warm area where temperature will remain even.
5. Rinse 2-3 times per day.
6. Once they reach the desired length, place near sunlight until leaves become green.

15 Ways To Use Sprouts

Sprouts are an excellent way to provide your family with fresh nutrients. Here are some ways you may not have thought of to use them.

1. Stir fry mung bean sprouts in sesame oil with mushrooms, scallions, grated ginger, and soy sauce.

2. Blend garbanzo bean sprouts, lemon juice, minced garlic, olive oil, salt, and pepper into a thick paste. Chill and serve on crackers for a healthy snack.

3. Combine soy bean sprouts, fresh corn kernels, and sliced red onions with an oil and vinegar dressing for a lively salad.

4. Save the water the sprouts initially soaked in for a nutritious soup base to mix with fruit juices or for watering house plants.

5. Make a wonderful sandwich with peanut butter and alfalfa sprouts.

6. Replace wild rice with rye sprouts in soups and rice combinations.

7. Chopped raw lentil sprouts give a peppery taste to cream cheese for a spread.

8. Combine raw mung bean sprouts with raisins, apple, and tomato slices, avocado, and cucumber chunks. Toss with a salad dressing.

9. Blend wheat sprouts, bananas, wheat germ, honey and milk to make a quick high energy drink.

10. Add alfalfa sprouts to scrambled eggs just before serving.

11. Chopped meats stretch further if you add fresh soybean sprouts. It really tastes even better with them added.

12. Stir fresh pea sprouts into a canned tomato soup for extra vitamins and flavor. The kids will never know they had their veggies.

13. Mix tuna with fresh sprouts, sliced apples, chopped mushrooms, lemon juice, salt, and pepper for an exciting low calorie lunch.

14. Keep sprouts on hand and add them whenever you add herbs and spices to meals.

15. You can always add sprouts to sandwiches instead of lettuce and on top of a salad to perk it up with spicy flavors such as mustard, radish, or a spicy sprout mix.

All About Meats

Meats are generally not included in basic Long Term Food Storage Calculators. It is expected that you will get your protein from legumes. However, if you can add some form of meat into your storage it opens up a lot more possibilities for making "normal" meals, can add dense calories/protein, and can help with avoiding flavor fatigue. Here are a few tips on storing meats:

- Buy smaller amounts to start until you are sure you like using that variety, preservation method, etc.
- Consider the shelf life on items and store accordingly.
- Practice using the foods to make sure they will make good substitutes in your meals when it comes time to use them.
- When choosing a preservation method, it helps to think through water necessities (for rehydration), power needs (if you are freezing meats), and space constraints.

In general it's a good idea to store meats in a variety of ways to take advantage of the pros and minimize the cons of each method.

Here is a summary of each type of meat preservation method you may want to consider for your storage.

CANNING MEATS FOR HOME STORAGE:

Pros of Canned Meats:
- Can be inexpensive after you have all the canning supplies
- Purchase meats on sale and preserve them
- Complete control over varieties and flavors you store
- Delicious and EASY to use
- No water necessary when preparing meals

Cons of Canned Meats:
- Short shelf life (1–2 years)
- Takes lots of time to preserve
- Can be intimidating, risk of not preserving properly
- Some meats may look/taste different than regular cooked meats

If you don't want to can your own meat you can also purchase a variety of canned meats from the grocery store which can be another great option for getting meat into your storage. Store-bought canned meat will be more expensive.

FREEZING MEATS FOR HOME STORAGE:

Freezing is a very common method for preserving meat. It is best accomplished using a vacuum sealer to avoid freezer burn. Many people choose to use freezer foods in their 3 month supply and plan to quickly cook or preserve the food should the power go out.

Pros of Freezer Meats:
• Can take advantage of sale prices
• Easy to do, does not take a lot of time
• Easy to incorporate the foods into regular recipes

Cons of Freezer Meats:
• Freezers are affected by power loss
• Limited amount of space available
• Shorter shelf life (6 months – 1 year)

DEHYDRATING MEATS FOR HOME STORAGE:

Dehydrating can be done at home with a food dehydrator. Dehydrated meats are basically just jerky. You can dehydrate meats yourself to make all kinds of different jerkys. You can also purchase jerky at the store.

Pros of Dehydrated Meats:
• Long shelf life if preserved properly
• Inexpensive after equipment is purchased
• Wide variety of flavors and meat varieties you can make

Cons of Dehydrated Meats:
• Not good for young children, too chewy
• Can be difficult and time consuming to dehydrate yourself
• Not useful for using in recipes as a substitution for fresh meats

FREEZE-DRIED MEATS FOR HOME STORAGE:

Purchasing freeze–dried meats is probably the easiest method for getting meats into your storage and you can be confident that they will last a long time. However, it is also the most expensive of the methods discussed here. There are home freeze-drying machines now available if you want to take on the expense and risk of doing it yourself.

Pros of Freeze-Dried Meats:
• 20–25 year shelf life
• Easy to store in large quantities
• Easy to substitute into regular recipes
• Commercially-preserved products eliminate safety concerns from home preservation

Cons of Freeze-Dried Meats:
• Must have water storage to rehydrate
• Expensive price-per-pound of meat
• They don't work in all meat recipes (i.e. chicken on a grill)

Using Freeze-Dried Meats

Since freeze-dried meats are new to some people, here are some examples of how to use it in your everyday cooking:

TOSS IT IN:

Any type of soup, stew, or sauce is liquid enough to reconstitute your meats within a few minutes. No need to hydrate them first. It is so easy and can add bulk and calories to any meal. No chopping, thawing, cooking, etc. required.

BULK IT UP:

Many just-add-water meals tend to be vegetarian in order to keep the price down. There are a lot of bean and rice meals, soups, etc. that hover around 200-300 calories per serving. If you have a lot of those type of meals in your storage, adding some freeze-dried meat can be a great supplement. You would want to rehydrate them in hot water, and then add them in just as your meal is almost finished cooking.

WRAP IT:

Don't have time to prepare some chicken for a quick enchilada or quesadilla? No problem! Add freeze-dried chicken and you can add some protein to your wrap in about 5 minutes. Dinner is fast and easy and you are practicing with (and rotating) your food storage.

TOP IT:

An excellent food storage meal to make is pizza using freeze-dried cheese. (Who will be sad in an emergency if you can eat pizza?) Freeze-dried chicken, beef, or sausage are all great pizza toppings to add some variety to your pizza.

EXTEND IT:

If you are running short on meat in your freezer/fridge, or you are worried about trying things with just freeze-dried meat, it is so easy to mix it half and half. It works to cook half a pound hamburger and throw in some reconstituted freeze-dried ground beef while it fries up. It can be used for tacos, sloppy joes, etc. and no one will even know it wasn't 100% fresh meat.

EAT IT DRY:

Ok this may sound a little odd but freeze-dried sausage crumbles dry can be delicious as a crunchy topping for a salad or in a mountain man mix with freeze-dried cheese and some seasonings. Think bacon bits but better.

BABYSTEP 7: BAKING INGREDIENTS

INTRODUCTION:

★ The ingredients in Step 7 are all the necessary fats, oils, sugars, milk, and miscellaneous items that you need to put food storage meals and recipes together.

★ Purchasing these items when on sale, then rotating through your stored supplies can save you time and money.

★ Find ways to use these ingredients in your everyday cooking, start learning how to make things from scratch.

★ Determine the quantities of each food item you will need to store. For more information see Long Term Food Storage Planning {found on page 83}.

★ Baking ingredient groups include:
- Fats and Oils
- Sugars
- Powdered Dairy
- Miscellaneous

INSIDE THIS SECTION:

All About Baking Ingredients
All About Powdered Milk
All About Powdered Eggs
All About Honey
All About Powdered Butter
All About Powdered Sour Cream
All About Freeze-Dried Cheese
All About Yeast & Gluten
Food Storage Substitutions

All About Baking Ingredients

FATS AND OILS:

Salad Dressings: Salad dressings can be store-bought and stored, or you can make your own oil and vinegar-based, or mayonnaise-based dressings with items you have on hand in your food storage. Be aware of expiration dates on store dressings.

Cooking Oil: Cooking oil such as canola or vegetable oil can be used in most bread recipes. Unless they have been specially treated, unopened cooking oils have a shelf life of about a year so be aware of rotating and replenishing.

Shortening: Shortening has a longer shelf life than oils. It is reasonable to expect an unopened metal can of shortening to have a shelf life of eight to ten years if kept fairly cool, particularly if it has preservatives in it. Powdered shortening is another option with a long shelf life and is great to use for baking.

Mayonnaise: Mayonnaise can be used in baked dishes, pasta salads, salad dressings, and much more. Although it isn't necessary to sustain life, it sure makes things taste better. Mayonnaise has a shelf life of 2-3 months.

Peanut Butter: Peanut butter provides protein and monounsaturated fats (the good fat). Peanut butter has a shelf life of 6-9 months.

POWDERED DAIRY:

Instant Powdered Milk: Instant powdered milk is most typically used for drinking. It reconstitutes better than non-instant milk.

Non-Instant Powdered Milk: This milk can be much cheaper than regular milk. It is typically used in baking. However, if you are drinking it, make it taste better by adding 1 tsp of sugar, and 1 tsp of vanilla per gallon, and refrigerate before drinking.

Evaporated Milk: Evaporated milk can be stored in cans, or made from nonfat dry milk. To make a 12 oz can of evaporated milk from dry milk, mix 1-1/2 C. Water and 1/2 C. + 1 T. Dry Powdered Milk and blend very well.

Powdered Eggs: These can be used to create a lot of different recipes that will help you have variety in your diet in an emergency. Historically they've cheaper than regular eggs so rotating them into your everyday cooking makes a lot of sense.

Butter: Butter can be purchased in powder or canned form. We don't recommend canning your own butter due to safety concerns, but commercially canned should be fine. Storing butter is not very cost-effective so we don't recommend storing a lot of it or making a large effort to rotate it into everyday cooking.

Sour Cream: Sour cream is available in powdered form. Some people may wish to keep a little on hand to use in family favorite recipes that call for sour cream.

SUGARS:

Powdered Fruit Drink: Powdered fruit drink comes in many different flavors and can be used in daily use and in times of emergency as stored water can have a funny taste. Powdered drink mixes can be stored for up to 3 years if unopened.

Brown Sugar: Brown sugar can be used in many baked goods and even some bread recipes. It can be stored up to 6 months. Some people store white sugar and molasses to make their own brown sugar, to avoid dealing with shelf life issues.

Molasses and Corn Syrup: These are used as sweeteners in many recipes. Store according to your family's needs. Molasses may be something you have never used, nor ever will use. If this is the case, don't feel the need to store it. If you choose not to store brown sugar, you will want to store more molasses in order to make your own.

Flavored Gelatin: This is used in molded desserts and salads.

Jams or Preserves: This is covered in BabyStep 8: Fruits & Vegetables {found on page 125}.

Granulated Sugar: Sugar is used in many food storage recipes and is very important to store. Sugar has a shelf life of 20+years.

Honey: Honey is another sweetener found in a lot of food storage recipes. It is more expensive than white sugar but is healthier so store according to your family's preferences and budget. You can store honey almost indefinitely, just heat it up if it gets crystalized. You can also store honey crystals which are useful in baking and to sprinkle on as a sweet topping.

MISCELLANEOUS:

Baking: Baking soda, salt and baking powder are used in most baked good recipes. Baking soda and salt if unopened, have indefinite shelf lives. Baking powder has a shelf life of 1-2 years but can be made by mixing 1 part baking soda with 2 parts cream of tartar (which also has an indefinite shelf life). Definitely make sure to keep these ingredients on hand for your favorite recipes.

Active Dry Yeast: Active dry yeast is the form of yeast most commonly available to non-commercial bakers, as well as the yeast of choice for emergency situations where uncontrolled storage conditions are likely.

Instant Yeast: Instant yeast is similar to active dry yeast, but has smaller granules with substantially higher percentages of live cells. It is more perishable than active dry yeast, but also does not require rehydration, and can usually be added directly to all but the driest doughs.

All About Powdered Milk

WHY STORE POWDERED MILK?

Food storage calculators generally recommend storing anywhere from16 pounds to 75 pounds of powdered milk per person. The 16 pound recommendation accounts for one glass of milk per day for a year. If you have small children it is important to have even more powdered milk. Because of the high nutrient levels in powdered milk, you can actually sustain life by drinking only powdered milk for quite some time.

INSTANT VS NON-INSTANT POWDERED MILK:

Instant powdered milk is similar to instant rice in that it is faster and easier to reconstitute than non-instant varieties. Typically instant powdered milk takes about twice as much powder per gallon as non-instant, but it depends on which brand you are purchasing.

WHAT IS MILK ALTERNATIVE:

A milk alternative is NOT 100% milk. It contains a lot of ingredients to make it taste better including whey, partially hydrogenated vegetable oil, and high fructose corn syrup. As a result, it tastes better but has less protein and includes some extra ingredients. Milk alternative can affect recipes differently than regular powdered milks due to the ingredients.

WHICH BRAND OF MILK TASTES BEST:

The Utah Preppers blog posted an in depth taste test on the most common brands of powdered milk available. According to their study, the best-tasting milks were: Morning Moos (Milk alternative), Provident Pantry (Instant powdered milk), and Rainy Day (Non-instant powdered milk). One trick to improve taste is to mix a little bit of sugar and vanilla into your powdered milk and then serve it cold.

OPTIONS BESIDES "NON-FAT" POWDERED MILK:

Dry whole milk is available although it's much more difficult to find, especially in bulk. One brand that is dry whole milk is Nido. You can often find it in the Hispanic foods section at your local grocery store. Or you might also find it available online at Amazon.com. It's more expensive than non-fat milk and the storage life will be much shorter due to the fat content of the milk so make sure to consider that.

SHELF LIFE AND ROTATION:

While different sources claim the shelf life on powdered milk can be up to 20-25 years, some reports show nutrient levels significantly drops within that time. It's a good idea to get in the habit of rotating your powdered milk to keep your supplies fresh.   If you don't enjoy drinking powdered milk make sure you use it in your recipes. Using powdered milk in recipes is a great way to rotate it and save money too.

All About Powdered Eggs

WHAT ARE POWDERED EGGS:

Powdered eggs are eggs that have been dehydrated and made into a simple granular powder. While some brands of powdered eggs utilize the whole egg, others will only include the yolks or the whites, or may add other ingredients to enhance the flavor or the texture of the reconstituted eggs. Generally, it is possible to purchase powdered eggs in bulk, making them ideal for use in food storage programs.

ADVANTAGES OF POWDERED EGGS:

Dehydrated eggs have several advantages over fresh eggs. First, powdered eggs have a long shelf life. With proper storage, dried eggs can easily last for the better part of a decade. It is not necessary to store the eggs in a refrigerated area, just in a cool and relatively dark location. Eggs that have been dried require much less storage space. This means substantial supplies of eggs can be kept on hand in a relatively small space. In powdered form, the eggs can be added to baked recipes without the need to mix them with a liquid ahead of time. They also are safe to eat raw, which makes them appealing to use in cookie recipes if you want to eat the dough.

USING POWDERED EGGS:

Today, powdered or dry types of eggs are available in several different ways. Whole eggs may be dehydrated and later used in many recipes where whole eggs are needed. For use in recipes where the whites are all that is used, such as in meringues, packages of powdered egg whites are available, although there is some difference of opinion as to how well powdered egg whites work and taste when utilized in some recipes. Scrambled egg mixes are also available if you want a product that is similar to cooked eggs.

HISTORY LESSON:

The production of powdered eggs is usually traced back to the first half of the 20th century. The eggs were extensively used during World War II, especially in countries where food supplies were airlifted in to feed civilians displaced by occupations and bombings. In the United States, powdered eggs were often used as a substitute for fresh eggs during periods of rationing, allowing fresh eggs to be routed to provide nutrition to people serving in the military. Even with first call on fresh eggs, many branches of the military also utilized the powdered versions as a matter of expediency.

Food Storage Made Easy

All About Honey

HOW MUCH HONEY TO STORE:

According to most food storage calculators it is recommended to store 60 pounds total of sugars/sweeteners per year per adult. The calculator in BabyStep 4 {found on pages 84-85}. uses the common recommendation of just 3 pounds of honey per person. However, if your basic bread recipe calls for honey, you may choose to store more than that.

Some people feel that for health reasons they would rather store more honey than refined white sugar so obviously they would also increase their honey storage amount. As you start using your food storage more and baking a lot from scratch you may find that you prefer to cook with honey and thus want to increase your storage amount for that reason as well.

DIFFERENT TYPES OF HONEY:

Raw: Unheated honey that has been removed from the comb. It may contain bits of wax, insect parts and other small debris. Raw honey contains small amounts of vitamins and minerals that are not in white sugar.

Filtered: Raw honey that has been warmed slightly to make it easier to filter out small particles and impurities. Filtered honey is almost the same as raw, just a little cleaner. Most of the small amounts of nutrients remain.

Liquid: Honey that has been heated to higher temperatures to allow for easier filtering and to kill any microorganisms. Usually lighter in color, this form is milder in flavor, resists crystallization and is generally clearer than raw honey. Much of the trace amounts of vitamins are lost in this processing.

Crystallized or Spun: This honey has had some of its moisture content removed to make a creamy spread. It is the most processed form of honey.

BENEFITS OF HONEY:

Reduce cough and throat irritation: Honey helps with coughs, particularly buckwheat honey.

Blood sugar regulation: Even though honey contains simple sugars, it is not the same as white sugar or artificial sweeteners. Its exact combination of fructose and glucose actually helps the body regulate blood sugar levels.

Heal wounds and burns: External application of honey has been shown to be as effective as conventional treatments.

Allergies: Raw local honey can help fight common allergies.

All About Powdered Butter

Most traditional long term food storage calculators do not cover items such as powdered butter, powdered sour cream, etc. These are not considered "life-sustaining" foods but they are considered useful additions to any food storage plan.

WHAT IS POWDERED BUTTER:

Powdered butter is a light powder that can be used to replace butter in a 1-1 substitution in most baking recipes. It generally has a 5 year shelf life in an unopened can.

HOW DO I USE POWDERED BUTTER:

If you have a recipe that calls for 1 cup of butter, you would replace that with 1 cup of powdered butter and 1 cup of water. Ratios may vary depending on the brand. You do not need to mix them together first. It normally works best to add the butter powder in with the dry ingredients, and the water in with the wet ingredients in your recipe. Some people recommend doing a slightly higher ratio than 1-1. So use 1 1/2 cups of powder and water if it calls for 1 cup of butter. Experiment with your recipes and see which way you prefer.

WILL MY RECIPES TURN OUT DIFFERENTLY:

Powdered butter tends to make things turn out a little lighter and fluffier. We recommend opening one of your cans and practicing with the butter powder in some of your favorite family recipes until you get the hang of how it will work and any adjustments you might need to make.

CAN I USE POWDERED BUTTER AS A SPREAD ON BREAD:

If you reconstitute according to the directions on the can, you will find that the butter is too runny to use for a good spreadable butter. Try using 1 T. butter powder, 1 tsp. water, 1 tsp. oil, and a dash of salt or sugar (depending on how you prefer your butter).

CAN I USE POWDERED BUTTER TO FRY FOODS:

No, powdered butter does not melt in the same way that regular butter melts so it will not work in recipes calling for melted butter to pan-fry your foods.

IS POWDERED BUTTER MORE EXPENSIVE THAN FRESH:

Prices vary on both fresh and powdered butter. In general the powdered form is going to be slightly higher priced than fresh butter. Because of this, it is not recommended to always use powdered butter in your everyday baking. You should however store some of it and use it enough to rotate (remember the 5 year shelf life) and to practice it in your own recipes until you feel comfortable using it.

All About Powdered Sour Cream

Most traditional long term food storage calculators do not cover items such as powdered butter, powdered sour cream, etc. These are not considered "life-sustaining" foods but can be useful additions to any food storage plan.

WHAT IS POWDERED SOUR CREAM:

Sour cream powder is a cream that has had the fat removed and is dehydrated in order to preserve it. It has a shelf life of about 10 years if stored in a sealed can at moderate temperatures.

HOW DO I USE POWDERED SOUR CREAM:

Powdered sour cream is wonderful for using in recipes. It gives a nice sour cream flavor and adds the creaminess to any recipe that calls for normal sour cream. Since the fat has been removed, it does not reconstitute to a nice thick creamy sour cream that you would use for tacos or nachos. The flavor is not quite right and the consistency isn't what you are used to.

HOW MUCH POWDERED SOUR CREAM EQUALS FRESH:

Sour cream powder is a cup for cup equivalent. So if you want a cup of sour cream, you would do one cup of the powder and then mix with whatever amount of water you need for your desired consistency.

WILL MY RECIPES TURN OUT DIFFERENTLY:

Depending on the brand you use, the directions on the can might yield a thicker or thinner sour cream than you are used to. Just adjust the water content to get it the consistency you desire and your recipes should turn out the same.

IS POWDERED SOUR CREAM MORE EXPENSIVE THAN FRESH:

There are about 13 cups in a #10 can. When comparing the price of the sour cream to fresh, look at the number of cups it will yield. Typically powdered sour cream will be more than a grocery store sour cream, but you won't be throwing out any leftovers because you can make just the right amount.

All About Freeze-Dried Cheese

One of the most critical aspects of building a food storage is to store foods that can be used in meals that your family will eat. So many family favorite recipes include cheese. Adding a little bit to your food storage will be a relief for those who are used to using cheese in many of their every day recipes.

WHAT IS FREEZE-DRIED CHEESE:

Freeze-dried cheese goes through the same flash freezing process that freeze-dried fruits and vegetables go through. First the cheese is frozen, then it is placed under vacuum. This enables the frozen liquid in the product to vaporize without passing through the liquid phase, a process known as sublimation. Heat is applied to the frozen product to accelerate sublimation. Low-temperature condenser plates remove the vaporized liquid from the vacuum chamber by converting it back to a solid. This completes the separation process. You are then left with a cheese product you can use like regular shredded cheese after you rehydrate it.

WHAT VARIETIES DOES FREEZE-DRIED CHEESE COME IN:

Most food storage companies sell one or several of four varieties of freeze-dried cheese. You can often find cheese blends but those are a powder and will not turn out like regular cheese at all. The four main varieties are: Cheddar Cheese, Mozzarella Cheese, Colby Cheese, Monterrey Jack Cheese.

IS FREEZE-DRIED CHEESE MORE EXPENSIVE THAN FRESH:

Freeze-dried cheese is a fairly expensive product compared to its fresh equivalent. We usually recommend that you try a few of your favorite recipes to make sure that you are comfortable with using it, but don't necessarily plan to replace your fresh cheese with it on a regular basis.

WHERE CAN I BUY FREEZE-DRIED CHEESE:

Most online stores that sell freeze-dried foods will sell freeze-dried cheese. It's a good idea to buy some smaller cans to test, and bigger cans for storage purposes.

WHAT ARE SOME RECIPES I CAN TRY:

Here are a types of recipes freeze-dried cheese works great in:
• omelets
• casseroles
• pizzas
• lasagnas
• pasta salads
• toppings on soups and chili

HOW DO I RECONSTITUTE FREEZE-DRIED CHEESE:

There are two methods for reconstituting your cheese.

Traditional method:

The traditional method will take a little longer, but it will turn out just like regular cheese.

1. Place 2 cups of freeze-dried cheese in a glass bowl.
2. With a spoon, lightly stir cheese while drizzling 1/2 cup of cold water over the cheese. Stir continuously until all the water is incorporated into the cheese.
3. Water should just barely start to collect on the bottom of the glass bowl. This is a sign that the cheese has absorbed enough water.
4. Place cheese in a zip lock bag and store in refrigerator overnight or for several hours before use.

Quick Method:

The quick method will turn out just fine for recipes where you will be melting the cheese in your finished product.

1. Place a thick layer of paper towels on a plate.
2. Pour dried cheese onto the paper towels.
3. Spray the cheese with a spray bottle and stir around with your finger.
4. Continue spraying and waiting a little bit, spraying and waiting.
5. Once water starts to pool under the paper towel, it should be pretty well hydrated. It may be slightly crunchy but should work fine in recipes for melting.

All About Yeast and Gluten

Since wheat is such a common staple of most people's food storage, it is critical to learn how to use it. The easiest thing to make (without storing a lot of ingredients) is bread. Two of the items common in bread recipes are yeast and vital wheat gluten.

ALL ABOUT YEAST:

What is yeast?

Yeast is a microscopic fungus that is used in baking for leavening purposes. The kind most people use for baking is Active Dry Yeast.

What Type of Yeast Should I Buy?

There are three types of active dry yeast, use whatever kind your recipe calls for or you will have differing results.
- Regular Active Dry Yeast: Requires "proofing" which means you add it to hot water and wait until it activates before combining with other ingredients. This type requires a double-rise typically.
- Instant Active Dry Yeast: Can be added in with the other dry ingredients in a recipe and then add liquid later because it has been milled into finer particles. This type can be used interchangeably with regular yeast in a recipe, you just skip the proofing step. Usually a double-rise is still required.
- Quick-Rising Instant Active Dry Yeast: Is similar to Instant Active Dry Yeast except enzymes and other additives are added to make it rise faster. This enables you to do a single rise for most recipes. This yeast acts and tastes different so it's not recommended in all recipes.

What is the Shelf Life of Yeast:

Yeast can store for 6 months to 1 year on the shelf, or longer than a year if you store it in the freezer. This can make it difficult to plan for long term food storage situations. We recommend testing the yeast to make sure it's still active and discard and replace if necessary to keep your "year supply" fully stocked.

How Do I Know if My Yeast is Still Active?

To test yeast, add 1 teaspoon sugar to 1/4 cup warm water (100° to 110°F). Stir in 1 envelope yeast (2 1/4 teaspoons); let stand 10 minutes. If the yeast foams to the 1/2 cup mark, it is active and you may use it in your recipe.

Info found at: http://www.breadworld.com/faq.aspx

What is Vital Wheat Gluten?

Vital Wheat Gluten functions as a "dough enhancer" in bread recipes. Gluten is the protein part of wheat flour and gives bread dough it's elasticity and the bread a nice shape. It also helps bind it together so that it is less crumbly. Vital Wheat Gluten is a powdered form for gluten which basically takes the positive properties of the gluten and enhances them when added to a bread recipe.

What is the Shelf Life of Vital Wheat Gluten?

Most Vital Wheat Gluten has a shelf life of 7-10 years if unopened and stored in ideal storage conditions. Once opened it should be used within 6 months to a year unless stored in the freezer to extend the shelf life.

Can I Use a Substitute for Vital Wheat Gluten?

Wheat Protein Isolate (from Honeyville Grain) is a suitable replacement for Vital Wheat Gluten – it's more concentrated and more expensive. You can use less of it to get the same results. Other bread recipes may use other dough enhancers to achieve similar results such as white vinegar, potato flakes, Vitamin C tablets, etc.

Food Storage Substitutions

When you are cooking a lot of foods from scratch, storing all the different ingredients can become overwhelming. Try storing fewer ingredients and making other ingredients from them. Here are some examples of make your own ingredients from common stored ingredients.

Ingredient	Amount	Substitution
Sweetened Condensed Milk	14 oz can	1/2 cup hot water 1 cup dry powdered milk 1 cup sugar 1 T butter Blend very well
Evaporated Milk	12 oz can	1 1/2 cup water 1/2 cup +1 T dry powdered milk Blend very well
Buttermilk	1 cup	1 cup prepared dry powdered milk 1 T of lemon juice or white vinegar Mix and let stand 10 mins
Brown Sugar	1 cup	1 cup granulated sugar 1/4 cup molasses Mix together
Chocolate, baking	1 oz. square	3 T cocoa powder 1 T butter Mix together
Baking Powder	1 tsp	1/4 tsp soda 5/8 tsp cream of tartar Mix together
Allspice	1 tsp	1/2 tsp cinnamon 1/2 tsp ground cloves Mix together
Pumpkin Pie spice	1 tsp	1/2 tsp cinnamon 1/4 tsp ginger 1/8 tsp allspice 1/8 tsp nutmeg Mix together

INTRODUCTION:

★ When looking at food storage calculators, you may notice fruits and vegetables are often left off. This is because you can sustain life with the ingredients on those calculators (you can sprout a number of those ingredients to get fresh vegetable sources). However, storing fruits and vegetables is good for the health benefits, variety, and to help you save money on your day to day grocery shopping.

★ Growing Your Own Fruits and Vegetables
- Growing your own foods is a great way to be self reliant.
- Our favorite method for growing vegetables is square foot gardening which allows you to grow a lot of veggies in a small space.
- If you have space, fruit trees and vines can be a great cost-savings.

★ Dehydrated or Freeze-Dried
- Dehydrated and freeze-dried fruit make snacks, smoothies, and desserts.
- Dehydrated and freeze-dried vegetables are wonderful additions to soups/stews. Items such as dehydrated onions can save you time and hassle in your cooking.
- You can purchase a food dehydrator or freeze-dryer to preserve some foods.
- Freeze-dried and dehydrated fruits and vegetables are safer and last longer if they are commercially packaged.

★ Canned/Bottled
- You can bottle a wide variety of things such as salsa, pie fillings, applesauce, juice, spaghetti sauce, almost any fruit or vegetable, pickles, and all sorts of jams.
- Canning your own fruits and vegetables can be a great money saver.
- Home-bottled foods have less preservatives, taste better, and you can adjust the amounts of sugar you use to fit your family's preferences.
- If you choose to purchase cans of fruits and vegetables, you can either purchase an extra few cans each time you shop until you have built up your year supply, or stock up when there are good sales.

★ Frozen
- Freezing produce takes much less time and preparation than home bottling and can be done using less sugar or other preservatives.
- If you don't have home-grown foods, you can purchase fresh produce in bulk to freeze, or simply buy bags of frozen fruits and vegetables on sale.

INSIDE THIS SECTION:

All About Dehydration
All About Freeze-Drying
All About Canning
All About Square Foot Gardening
How To Build A Vinyl Square Foot Garden Box

All About Food Dehydration

WHAT IS DEHYDRATING:

Drying is the oldest method of preserving food. The early American settlers dried foods such as corn, apple slices, currants, grapes, and meat. Compared with other methods, drying is quite simple. In fact, you may already have most of the equipment on hand. Dried foods keep well because the moisture content is so low that spoilage organisms cannot grow.

DEHYDRATING VS CANNING AND FREEZING:

Drying will never replace canning and freezing because these methods do a better job of retaining the taste, appearance, and nutritive value of fresh food. But drying is an excellent way to preserve foods that can add variety to meals and provide delicious, nutritious snacks. One of the biggest advantages of dried foods is that they take much less storage space than canned or frozen foods.

DEHYDRATION METHODS:

Recommended methods for canning and freezing have been determined by research and widespread experience. Home drying, however, does not have firmly established procedures. Food can be dried several ways, for example, by the sun if the air is hot and dry enough, or in an oven or dryer if the climate is humid. With the renewed interest in gardening and natural foods and because of the high cost of commercially-dried products, drying foods at home is becoming popular again. Drying is not difficult, but it does take time and a lot of attention. Although there are different drying methods, the guidelines remain the same.

Although solar drying is a popular and very inexpensive method, some areas do not have a suitable climate for it. Dependable solar dehydration of foods requires 3 to 5 consecutive days when the temperature is 95 degrees F. and the humidity is very low.

Drying food in the oven of a kitchen range, on the other hand, can be very expensive. In an electric oven, drying food has been found to be nine to twelve times as costly as canning it. Food dehydrators are less expensive to operate but are only useful for a few months of the year. A convection oven can be the most economical investment if the proper model is chosen. A convection oven that has a controllable temperature starting at 120 degrees F. and a continuous operation feature rather than a timer-controlled one will function well as a dehydrator during gardening months. For the rest of the year it can be used as a tabletop oven.

*This information is taken from the University of Illinois at Urbana-Champaign, College of Agriculture, Cooperative Extension Service, Circular 1227. For even more detailed information please visit their website at http://www.aces.uiuc.edu/vista/html_pubs/ DRYING/dryfood.html

All About Freeze-Drying

Many people think that freeze-dried foods are the same as dehydrated. However, there are some significant differences between the two processes as well as a big difference in the finished product. Let's explore the freeze-drying process in more depth.

FREEZE-DRYING PROCESS:

This description of the freeze-drying process comes from Thrive Life, a leading producer of freeze-dried foods.

1. Freezing: The product is frozen. This provides a necessary condition for low temperature drying.
2. Vacuum: After freezing, the product is placed under vacuum. This enables the frozen liquid in the product to vaporize without passing through the liquid phase, a process known as sublimation.
3. Heat: Heat is applied to the frozen product to accelerate sublimation.
4. Condensation: Low-temperature condenser plates remove the vaporized liquid from the vacuum chamber by converting it back to a solid. This completes the separation process.

BENEFITS OF FREEZE-DRIED FOODS:

HEALTHY: Freeze-drying retains a large percentage of the nutrients from the fresh item. It is the healthiest of all preservation methods.

SHELF LIFE: Since the freeze-drying process removes more moisture than dehydrating, the end result is a food item that has a longer shelf life. Most freeze-dried items can last up to 30 years on the shelf.

LIGHT-WEIGHT: Dehydrated foods shrivel and become compacted so a #10 can of dehydrated food is very heavy. Freeze-dried foods are the same size as their fresh counterpart, but are a fraction of the weight since all of the moisture is removed. This is beneficial for 72 hour kits when pack weight is a concern, but it takes up more space than an equivalent amount of dehydrated foods.

RETAINS ORIGINAL PROPERTIES: Freeze-dried foods retain their original shape, size, color, flavor, texture, etc. They can be eaten dry or reconstituted. When reconstituted they will be very similar to the fresh item.

EASY TO USE: Freeze-dried foods reconstitute very quickly and do not require cooking. Most dehydrated foods take a long time to rehydrate into a usable form. By using freeze-dried you will save on fuel costs and cook time.

FLAVORFUL: Freeze-dried fruits and vegetables are delicious straight out of the can. They give you a delicious natural flavor and don't contain all of the preservatives or flavorings that many dehydrated foods do.

All About Canning

Here are some tips to get started with canning your own foods.

GET A GOOD CANNING GUIDE:

Ball has published several canning books that are very helpful. A favorite go-to manual is the Ball Complete Book of Home Preserving. If there is anything you are thinking of canning, there should be instructions in there for you. Make sure to take note of the sections on altitudes as you may find that your processing times are different if you live in a very high (or low) area.

Another book which has more step-by-step instructions, beautiful photography, and personal tips, is <u>Yes, You Can! And Freeze and Dry It, Too</u> by Daniel Gasteiger. It's really fun to sit and browse through, and great for seeing instructions laid out very clearly.

Your pressure canner also should come with a booklet with details on processing times for that particular machine. That's a great resource to use as well.

GET YOUR CANNING TOOLS:

Water Bath Canner and/or Pressure Canner:
If you are planning to process high acid fruits and vegetables all you need is a basic water bath canner. If you want to process meats, beans, and some vegetables, you will need a pressure canner.

Canning Lids:
For all canning projects you must have canning lids and rings. This can be an expensive part of canning because you are supposed to buy new lids every time. At $4-$5 per box of 12 that can really add to the expense of one jar of food. Some people like to use Tattler Reusable Canning Lids. These are great since you don't have to throw them away after only one use.

Canning Jars:
A lot of retailers offer canning jars during canning season. Another great place to look is at garage sales or second hand stores. If you buy new jars it's nice because they come with lids and rings. If you are going to use the Tattler Reusable Lids you'll need enough rings for a few batches since you process the jars using rings, and leave them on while the jars cool. You can also find jars at a reasonable price on Amazon.

Optional Tools:
You can buy extra tools that you may want to have on hand such as tongs, a large funnel, a lid lifter, etc. which will make your canning tasks much easier.

All About Square Foot Gardening

Here are some of the most frequently asked gardening questions answered by Emily from MySquareFootGarden.net. There are a lot of benefits to growing a garden and becoming more self reliant.

WHAT SOIL MIX IS BEST FOR RAISED BED GARDENS:

I suggest a combination of ingredients called Mel's Mix. It is equal parts compost, vermiculite, and peat moss. Each spring I add more compost to my boxes—I usually need to add one quarter to one third of the volume of my garden bed. Also, after harvesting you can replant in that square. Before you do, add a scoop of compost and mix it in.

TELL ME MORE ABOUT SEEDS:

Do higher quality seeds really make a difference?
YES! I've personally experienced this. You know those super cheap seeds by American Seed Company? There's a reason they are so inexpensive. They have a very low germination rate, about 10%, which means you are paying for a bunch of seeds that won't sprout.

Where do you buy your seeds?
I have always purchased whatever brand I find at Wal-Mart, Home Depot, or IFA (Intermountain Farmers Association, the local farm coop store). I have found all of these seeds to be similarly priced and comparable in quality. The advantage of buying seeds at a local store (like IFA) is that they often carry brands that have been developed specifically for the climate in which you live. The advantage of purchasing from a catalog is that you can choose from endless varieties and types of vegetables. I just hate waiting for something to come in the mail!

What are Heirloom seeds?
Heirloom seeds, or vegetables, are varieties that were grown in the "old days." Many have been used for over 50 or 100 years, and there are many more varieties. However, they are not as disease-resistant as the seeds you will find at the store. Since the industrialization of agriculture, seeds have been bred for consistency and disease resistance. This has resulted in fewer varieties (sort of a "one size fits all") and hybrids, which are more expensive. Typically it is not recommended to store seeds from your home-grown vegetables to use the next year unless they are heirloom seeds.

How do I store seeds?
If you use the square foot gardening method, chances are you'll have tons of seeds leftover. I put mine in snack size ziplock baggies, so if the seeds spill out it's no big deal. Then I keep them in a cool, dry place. In the summer I put them in my fridge or basement. In the winter I keep them in the garage.

WHAT ARE GOOD PLANTS FOR COLDER CLIMATES:

Root veggies (beets, carrots, onions, leeks, turnips, radishes, potatoes)
Cabbage family (cabbage, broccoli, cauliflower, kale, mustard)
Peas and beans. If you have a short growing season, buy varieties that harvest in a shorter time frame.

COMPOSTING TIPS FOR BEGINNERS:

Don't do it. Okay, that's not totally true. If you have the space and want to compost for environmental reasons, by all means go ahead. But unless you have a lot of mass (think 100 gallons) and are willing to do a lot of work (turn it every week), you won't be generating compost for this year.

The only composting I know of that is compact, very little work, but does use food scraps (fruits and veggies only), is vermacomposting—that's right, with worms. I have a friend who does this. The compost she gets is like gold, but is measured in cups, not cubic feet.

ROTATING YOUR GARDEN PLANS:

If you do square foot gardening and use compost or Mel's mix, you will need to replenish it with compost every year. As long as you didn't have any diseases, there is no need to rotate your crops, unless you get bored, like me, or become obsessed with finding the perfect gardening layout (also like me).

PLANTS IN DESERT CLIMATES:

Most plants are ok in desert climates. You may have a hard time with cool-weather plants like broccoli, spinach, and peas. But if you give them an early start and shade from the hot sun, even these will grow well. Things like tomatoes and peppers do particularly well, since they can tolerate some heat and love the sunshine. I suggest everyone do a little research on their local extension website (www.extension.org) and/ or check out a local farming supply store for varieties developed specifically for your climate.

FERTILIZING:

I believe in fertilizing. This can be organic or chemical, but I don't feel Mel's mix provides sufficient nutrients for my gardens. Now, you have to be careful because if you fertilize with too much nitrogen you will have big, leafy plants and little fruit. I sometimes use an all-purpose fertilizer (20-20-20 or 10-10-10), but I really love one called Blooming and Rooting (9-59-8). I use it when starting seeds (about 4 weeks after germination) and on all my veggies that flower (squash, peas, beans, tomatoes, peppers) every 6 weeks.

How To Build A Garden Box

MATERIALS/TOOLS NEEDED:

- 4"x4" vinyl post jackets (found in either 72" or 100" lengths)
- Vinyl fence slats (found in 16' lengths)
- Fence post caps and liquid nails (optional)
- Tape measure
- Pencil
- Straight Edge/Ruler
- Table Saw (to cut vinyl into segments), Jigsaw (to cut the post holes)

INSTRUCTIONS:

Posts:
Measure post lengths to give you 1-2 inches of space at the top, and 4-6 inches of space at the bottom. Then give yourself either 5 1/2 or 11 inches for the slats (depending on whether you are doing one layer or two). Cut 4 equal segments. If you are doing a longer box, you will need to add 2 additional posts to give it more stability in the middle.

Side Slats:
Determine the size of box you want to make. For a 4 foot square box you would ideally give yourself a few extra inches on each side since they will be stuck into the posts. However, since the slats come in 16 foot lengths we opted to just make our box a little smaller. Cut into 4 equal segments. Again if you are doing a longer box, make additional slats as necessary. Don't make the slats longer than 4 or 5 feet in length.

Post Holes:
Draw yourself a template for the holes. Start down 1-2 inches from the top of the post (depending on what you measured for). Make sure to mark the center of the post. Measure your fence slat (should be about 1 1/2 inches) and mark that width down the post starting from the center. So you will have 3/4" on each side of the middle line. You can either measure 11" and draw the lines, or simply trace around your fence slat to get a pretty good outline. Use a large drill bit to start a hole in the outline. Then using a jigsaw, cut out the hole. You will need two holes per post and they should be on sides right next to each other.

Assembly:
If you glued your two layers of slats together, wait for them to dry. Then stick the fence slats into the holes you made in the posts and form your square foot garden box. Once you determine where your box will go, dig holes in the ground for the four post holes and stick your box in! We like to fill our posts with dirt after to make them more stable. Then stick on the post caps for a beautiful finishing touch.

Online Video Instructions:
View a video tutorial online at http://www.youtube.com/watch?v=Rbe3lRp_M68

BABYSTEP 9: COMFORT FOODS

INTRODUCTION:

★ Comfort foods can help ease your stress during rough times.

★ While not considered "life-sustaining" foods, we consider them "sanity-sustaining" foods. This is especially important if you have young children. A few normal foods or delicious snacks now and then can really help a difficult situation.

★ Use what you store, and store what you eat applies to comfort foods as well. Try a new thing each week or month. Some of these ideas may not be your normal treats but they are great food storage items.

★ Comfort Food Ideas
  • Home-made popcorn in a pot
  • Mashed potatoes with instant potatoes and gravy
  • Hard candy
  • Chocolate
  • Pudding (made using dry milk)
  • Granola bars
  • Fruit snacks for children
  • Chicken noodle soup in a can (for if you get sick)
  • Kool-aid
  • Condiments (ketchup, mustard, bbq sauce, salsa, pickles)
  • Spices (inventory what spices you use and store an extra one or two of each)
  • No-bake cookies
  • Rice Krispie Treats
  • Macaroni & cheese dinners
  • Chocolate and butterscotch baking chips for homemade cookies or snacking
  • Peppermint tea bags
  • Ovaltine
  • Homemade desserts

INSIDE THIS SECTION:

All About Spices And Condiments

All About Spices and Condiments

It's a good idea to get a few spare bottles of spices/herbs and condiments that you commonly use. This will ensure you have enough for your long term cooking needs, and also gives you the convenience and cost-savings in the short term. Don't go overboard on buying too many bottles though, as spices can lose their flavor over time.

COMMON HERBS:

Herbs are the leafy, green plant parts used for flavoring purposes and may be used fresh or dried, typically cut into very small pieces.

Basil
Leaves
Cilantro
Mint
Parsley
Sage
Thyme

Bay
Chives
Dill
Oregano
Rosemary
Tarragon

COMMON SPICES:

Spices are dried and often ground or grated into a powder. Small seeds, such as fennel and mustard seeds, are used both whole and in powder form

Allspice
Pepper
Cardamom
Chili Powder
Cloves
Cumin
Garlic Powder
Nutmeg
Salt
Red pepper flakes
Turmeric

Black
Caraway
Celery Salt/Seed
Cinnamon
Coriander
Fennel
Mustard Seed/Dry Mustard
Onion Powder
Paprika
Saffron
Vanilla

COMMON CONDIMENTS:

Ketchup
Relish
Peanut Butter
Soy Sauce
Teriyaki Sauce
Vinegar
Cranberry Sauce
Hot Sauce/Chili Sauce

Mustard
Mayonnaise
Barbecue Sauce
Worcestershire Sauce
Olive Oil
Horseradish
Applesauce
Taco Seasoning

BABYSTEP 10: NON-FOOD ITEMS

★ Store a year's supply of all household items that you normally buy at the grocery store.

★Build up your supply by buying these items in large quantities when they are on sale, then only replace your supplies when they go on sale again.

★ Make sure you store the things particular to your family's needs, our list might not include everything that you normally use.

★ Don't be afraid to use creative storage ideas for these items. A huge supply of toilet paper could go in a garage, attic, etc.

★ **Personal Hygiene:** Toothpaste/Toothbrushes, Shampoo/Conditioner, Deodorant, Facewash/Bodywash/Soap, Shaving/Aftershave

★ **Paper Products:** Toilet Paper, Paper Towels, Feminine Products, Diapers/Wet Wipes, Kleenex, Paper Plates/Plastic Utensils/Napkins (can save on water in an emergency)

★ **Cleaning Products:** Laundry Detergent, Dishwasher Detergent, Bleach, All-Purpose Cleaner, Items to make your own household cleaners

★ **First Aid Items:** First Aid Kits, Hand Sanitizer, Face Masks, Prescription Medications, Cold Medicine, Natural Medicines, Essential Oils

★ **Pet Care Products:** Dog/Cat Food, Extra Water for Pets, Kitty Litter

★ **Miscellaneous Items:** Light Bulbs, Board Games/Cards (something to do in case the power is out), Candles/Kerosene Lamps, Needles/Thread (for basic mending)

INSIDE THIS SECTION:

Basic First Aid

Basic First Aid

Having a basic understanding of First Aid should be a part of any emergency preparedness plan. It is a good idea to take CPR courses that are offered in your community. Here are some notes from a First Aid class to use as a starting point.

"NEW" CPR GUIDELINES:

There have been some changes to what the American Heart Association recommends for people to know about performing CPR. Since 2008 they have been encouraging all Americans to learn Hands-Only CPR in order to be able to potentially save the life of someone in cardiac arrest. The American Heart Association website says: Hands-Only CPR (CPR with just chest compressions) has been proven to be as effective as CPR with breaths in treating adult cardiac arrest victims.

To view the official video type this into your browser: http://youtu.be/zSgmledxFe8

Additional notes on CPR

- For small children use one hand only and compress only about half the distance from your hand to the ground.
- For infants only use 2 fingers.
- The first two compressions will be difficult and feel a bit "crunchy" as the ribs break away from cartilage, it should get easier after that.
- Don't stop doing compressions until a doctor pronounces them dead or someone with higher training takes over.
- Don't check for a pulse or for breathing before you start, just start compressions immediately after calling 911. Precious time is lost otherwise.

WHAT TO DO FOR CHOKING:

Try to determine if it is a partial obstruction or a complete obstruction. If it's partial, the object should be able to work its way out and the person is still able to breathe slightly. There is nothing you can do for this. If it is a complete obstruction, perform the Heimlich maneuver. This is done by wrapping your arms around the person, placing your thumb on their belly button, then making a fist and wrapping your other hand around that fist. Pull up and back until the obstruction is removed. If the person goes unconscious, perform CPR.

WHAT TO DO FOR HEAD TRAUMA:

If a person (usually a child) falls or receives some trauma to the head, check for the seriousness of the injury. If they are vomiting, go unconscious, act strange, get lethargic, or have a dramatic difference in pupil sizes these are all signs of a serious injury. If any of these symptoms occur, take the person to a doctor.

WHAT TO DO FOR SEVERE BLEEDING:

Call 911 if the cut is gushing, very deep, or a gaping wound.
Do your best to stop or minimized the bleeding. If you are using a rag or towel to stop the bleeding, make sure to sterilize it first. You can attempt to stop the bleeding in one of three ways:
• Apply pressure, either directly (push right on the injury) or indirectly (wrap a towel around the injury)
• Use pressure points. Find any place you feel a heart beat near the wound and apply pressure (i.e. under the bicep)
• Elevate the injury

Once you have stopped the bleeding, do not remove the towel to check on the injury. Wait until medical help arrives or you get to a hospital.

WHAT TO DO FOR POISONING:

If you have ANY concerns about what a person (or pet) has eaten, call poison control immediately. The phone number is 1-800-222-1222.

WHAT TO DO FOR HEAT EMERGENCIES:

Heat affects the young, old, and already sick much more than normal healthy adults. Heat exhaustion is quite common and is recognized by cool and clammy skin, nausea, and dizziness. Get the person out of the sun, keep them cool, and have them drink lots of water. If heat exhaustion is not treated quickly, it can develop into heat stroke which is very dangerous. Signs of heat stroke are red skin, radiating heat, becoming incoherent or unconscious, and the body can't control its temperature. This can be deadly, get medical attention immediately.

PART THREE

RECIPE APPENDIX

Welcome to the Food Storage Made Easy Recipe Appendix. This appendix includes recipes featured in our Food Storage Made Easy BabySteps Checklists. These recipes will help you try a wide variety of food storage foods. We also give you tips for converting your own recipes to food storage, and teach you some new food storage concepts. Sometimes using food storage foods can take a little practice, so if at first you don't succeed, try again.

Table of Contents

Food Storage Substitutions
Food Storage Equivalents

Recipes:

Food Storage Substitutions

When learning to use your food storage, one of the best things to do is learn how to convert your own family recipes into "food storage recipes". If you learn how to do this, then when an emergency situation arises you can have confidence to know you can cook meals that your family will like and that you have all of the ingredients for.

GENERAL RECOMMENDATIONS:

We recommend swapping out only one ingredient at a time in a recipe so that if it doesn't work out or your family complains about it, you can isolate that ingredient as the problem.

Don't be afraid to tweak measurements to get the consistency you want. Many recipes need the sour cream or butter to be thicker so you would want to use less water. It takes some trial and error to get it right for your specific recipes.

Any of the recipes in our appendix that call for substitutions are ones that we have tried and know work for our families, so you can feel confident in using them although your family's preferences may differ slightly. Here are a few tips and tricks for substituting food storage items in for regular ingredients:

Grains: In general, if a recipe calls for 1 cup of flour you can plan to use about ¾ cup of the grain to get the 1 cup in flour. It's best to try half and half with all-purpose flour rather than substitute 100% whole wheat right away.

Legumes: When grinding legumes expect a similar ratio to grains. Make sure you cook dry bean powder for at least 3 minutes for safety reasons if using as a soup or thickener.

Powders: When substituting powdered ingredients into your recipes, it works best to add the powder in with the dry ingredients and the liquid in with the wet ingredients. No need to reconstitute them first.

Freeze-Dried Fruits and Veggies: If you are cooking something with a lot of liquid you can just stick the freeze-dried items in without reconstituting first. If using as a topping or in a salad, follow reconstitution recommendations on the can.

Freeze-Dried Meats: If your recipe calls for the meat to be browned first, you can brown the freeze-dried meat without reconstituting. Just stick it in the pan with butter/oil for a few minutes. Then add water to the pan and reconstitute. This will give it the browned flavor as though it were fresh meat or chicken browned.

Freeze-Dried Cheese: You can either reconstitute it by spraying with water until it isn't crunchy any more, or you can soak in a small amount of water and then let sit overnight. The overnight method results in a product more similar to fresh cheese, but the spray method is faster.

Food Storage Equivalents Chart

Grains	
1 cup wheat kernels	1 ½ cups whole wheat flour
1 cup flour	~ ¾ cup wheat kernels
1 cup popcorn kernels	1 ½ cups cornmeal
1 cup cornmeal	~ ¾ cup popcorn kernels

Legumes	
4 T. dried white beans	5 T. white bean flour
15 oz can of beans	½ cup dry beans 1 ½ cups cooked beans
1 lb of dry beans	2 cups dry beans 6 cups cooked beans

Vegetables	
1 small onion	¼ cup dehydrated onion or ½ cup freeze-dried onion
3 stalks celery	½ cup freeze-dried celery
1 bell pepper	½ cup dehydrated peppers 1 cup freeze- dried peppers
1 cup chopped vegetables	⅓ cup dehydrated vegetables 1 cup freeze-dried vegetables

Fruits	
1 apple	1 cup freeze-dried apples
1 banana	1 cup freeze-dried bananas
1 cup berries (raspberry, strawberry, etc.)	1 cup freeze-dried berries
1 peach	1 cup freeze-dried peaches
1 cup pineapple	1 cup freeze-dried pineapple

Meats	
1 lb chicken or meat	1 ½ c. freeze-dried chicken or meat 1 pt home-canned chicken or meat

Cheese	
1 cup cheese	1 cup freeze-dried cheese, must reconstitute first for melting

Milk	
1 cup milk	3 T. powdered milk + 1 c. water
14 oz can sweetened condensed milk	½ c. hot water, 1 c. powdered milk, 1 c. sugar, 1 T. butter – Blend very well
12 oz can evaporated milk	1 ½ c. water, ½ c. + 1 T. powdered milk – Blend very well
1 cup buttermilk	1 T. lemon juice or white vinegar, 3 T. powdered milk, 1 c. water – Let sit 5 mins

Other	
1 egg	1 T. powdered egg + 2 T. water
1 cup sour cream	1 c. sour cream powder + 1 c. water
1 cup butter	1 c. butter powder + 1 c. water

12 Bean Soup

Ingredients:
2 c. 12-bean soup mix*
1 ham bone (optional)
4 T. BBQ sauce
1 chopped onion (can use food storage substitution, see chart)
1 T. sugar
1 small clove garlic
3 stalks celery, diced (can use food storage substitution, see chart)
¼ tsp. lemon pepper
2 carrots, diced (can use food storage substitution, see chart)
2 T. ketchup
28 oz. can whole tomatoes
¼ tsp. salt and ginger
1 pinch red pepper flakes
*You can buy this as a mix or make your own with legumes in your food storage

Directions:
Wash 2 cups of bean mix. Soak in a large pot overnight. Drain. Add 8 cups water, ham bone, 1 tsp. salt, and ¼ tsp. ginger. Bring to a boil and cook until beans are tender (about 1 hour). Add remaining ingredients. Bring to a boil. Simmer 2 ½ to 3 hours. Stir and add water as needed. For more zest, double all spices.

Baked Oatmeal

Ingredients:
2 c. quick oats
½ c. brown sugar
⅓ c. raisins
1 T. chopped pecans
1 tsp. baking powder
1 ½ c. skim milk (can use food storage substitution, see chart)
½ c. applesauce
2 T. butter, melted
1 large egg, beaten (can use food storage substitution, see chart)

Directions:
Preheat the oven to 375 degrees. Combine the first five ingredients in a medium bowl. If using dry milk and dry eggs, add those powders to the dry ingredients. Combine the milk (or water), applesauce, butter, and egg (or water) in a separate bowl. Add wet mixture to dry ingredients; stir well. Pour into a greased 8" square baking dish. Bake for 20-25 minutes or until just set. Makes 4-5 servings.

Basic Meatball Recipe

Ingredients:
1 lb ground beef (can use food storage substitution, see chart)
⅓ c. milk (can use food storage substitution, see chart)
½ c. fine dry bread crumbs
¼ c. dehydrated onion
1 egg (can use food storage substitution, see chart)
1 tsp. salt

Directions:
Mix all ingredients together. Shape into meatballs (it's easiest with a melon or ice cream scoop) and put on a rack with a pan underneath. Cover the pan with tinfoil to save on clean-up time. Bake at 425 for about 15 minutes. This recipe freezes well once baked.

Beach Street Lemon Chicken Linguine

Ingredients:
1 lb linguine (or fettuccine)
2 T. olive oil
Zest from one lemon
Juice from one lemon
½ c. chopped green onion (can use food storage substitution, see chart)
¼ c. chopped fresh parsley (can use food storage substitution, see chart)
Salt and freshly ground pepper
Parmesan cheese

Marinade:
½ c. olive oil
2 cloves garlic, whole
2 T. cajun seasoning
2 T. lemon juice
2 T. minced parsley (can use food storage substitution, see chart)
1 T. brown sugar
2 T. soy sauce
2 chicken breasts, sliced (can use food storage substitution, see chart)

Directions:
Combine the marinade ingredients in a Ziploc bag. Add sliced chicken. Refrigerate 1-12 hours. Cook marinated chicken with the marinade sauce in a large saute pan. Cook linguini in boiling water. Drain noodles. Combine juice of one lemon, zest, olive oil, green onions, and fresh parsley together to the noodles. Add in chicken and salt and pepper. Toss in parmesan cheese to taste and serve warm. *Recipe from Deals to Meals

Best Rice Krispie Squares

Ingredients:
½ c. white sugar
1 c. corn syrup
¾ c. peanut butter
2 c. Rice Krispies
4 c. Corn Flakes

Directions:
Use a large pot and stir together first three ingredients until melted & smooth. Do not overcook. Once you have a nice mixture, still in the cereal. You will want your pot to be big enough. Spread in a 9×13 pan.

Best Whole Wheat Bread Recipe

Ingredients:
7 c. whole wheat flour (fresh ground is best)
⅔ c. vital wheat gluten
2 ½ T. instant yeast
5 c. hot water (120-130 F)

2 T. salt
⅔ c. oil
⅔ c. honey
2 ½ T. bottled lemon juice
5 c. whole wheat flour

Directions:
Mix together the first three ingredients in your mixer with a dough hook. Add water all at once and mix for 1 minute; cover and let rest for 10 minutes (this is called sponging). Add salt, oil, honey, and lemon juice and beat for 1 minute. Add last flour, 1 cup at a time, beating between each cup. Beat for about 6-10 minutes until dough pulls away from the sides of the bowl. This makes very soft dough. Spray counter with Pam and take dough out of the bowl. Do NOT flour your counter, this will add dryness you don't want in the bread. You basically want your dough to feel a "little" sticky. Separate dough. Form into loaves and place in bread pans. Let rise until double in size. Bake at 350 for 22-30 mins or until browned. Makes 6 small to medium loaves. *Recipe from Deals to Meals.

Blackberry Pie

Pie Crust:
2 c. flour
1 T. salt
¾ c. butter flavored shortening
1 T. egg powder
¾ c. cold water
Blackberry Filling:
5-6 c. freeze-dried blackberries, rehydrated and drained
1 T. lemon juice
¾ c. white sugar
3 T. corn starch
⅛ tsp. cinnamon

Instructions:
Combine flour and salt. Cut in the shortening until the mixture is crumbly. Combine the egg powder and water. Add to the flour mix and stir until dough is formed. This makes a soft, sticky dough. Split into two pieces. Refrigerate for an hour for easier rolling. Roll out half the dough on a floured surface and place into a 9" pie crust. Return to fridge. Hydrate and drain blackberries, mix with lemon juice. Combine the other ingredients in a bowl and pour in the blackberries. Mix it all around and pour into the pie shell. Roll out the other half of the dough and cut it into 1 inch slices. Lay in a criss-cross pattern. Mix up a tiny bit of powdered milk with about twice the amount of powder as it normally calls for. Brush over top of the crust and then sprinkle with white sugar. Cover the edges with tinfoil and bake at 425 for about 30 minutes or until the crust is golden brown.

Blender Wheat Pancakes

Ingredients:
1 c. milk (can use food storage substitution, see chart)
1 c. wheat kernels, whole & uncooked
2 eggs (can use food storage substitution, see chart)
2 tsp. baking powder
1 ½ tsp. salt
2 T. oil
2 T. honey or sugar

Directions
Put milk and wheat kernels in blender. Blend on highest speed for 4 or 5 minutes or until batter is smooth. Add eggs, oil, baking powder, salt and honey or sugar to above batter. Blend on low. Pour out batter into pancakes from the actual blender jar onto a hot greased or Pam prepared griddle or large frying pan. Cook; flipping pancakes when bubbles pop and create holes.

Brown Sugar

Ingredients:
1 c. white sugar
1-2 T. molasses

Directions:
Use this recipe if you are out of brown sugar. This brown sugar can be made right before use, so there is no worry of having your brown sugar harden and become unusable. Mix sugar and molasses together. Depending on how dark you want the sugar, add more or less molasses.

Buttermilk Cornbread

Ingredients:
½ c. butter (can use food storage substitution, see chart)
⅔ c. white sugar
2 eggs (can use food storage substitution, see chart)
1 c. buttermilk {see powdered milk substitution found on page 140}
½ tsp. baking soda
1 c. cornmeal (grind your own with popcorn kernels)
1 c. all-purpose flour (works with whole wheat too)
½ tsp. salt

Directions:
Preheat oven to 375 degrees. Grease an 8 inch square pan. In a large bowl combine melted butter and white sugar. Quickly add eggs and beat until well blended. Combine buttermilk with baking soda and stir into mixture in pan. Stir in cornmeal, flour, and salt until well blended and few lumps remain. Pour batter into the prepared pan. Bake in the preheated oven for 25 to 30 minutes, or until a toothpick inserted in the center comes out clean.

Cheesy Ritzy Potatoes

Ingredients:
4 c. freeze-dried potato dices
⅓ c. dehydrated onion flakes
2 cans cream of chicken soup
1 c. sour cream powder, hydrated
¾ c. freeze-dried cheddar cheese
½ c. powdered butter, hydrated
2 tubes ritz crackers crushed

Directions:
Preheat your oven to 350 degrees. Soak your potato dices and dehydrated onions in warm water. In a separate bowl, soak your freeze-dried cheddar cheese. While they are soaking, mix up your sour cream powder with water. Stir in your cream of chicken soup. Drain your potatoes and pour them into a 9×13 casserole dish. Drain the rehydrated cheese and add it to the cream mixture. Pour the cream mixture over top of the potatoes and stir together well. In a small bowl mix up your powdered butter. Add the crushed ritz and mix well. Cover the dish with tinfoil and bake for 30-40 minutes. You can remove the foil for the last 5 minutes to get the topping more browned. While this works with powdered butter it's better and easier with regular melted butter.

Chicken Barley Chili

Ingredients:
1 (14.5 oz) can Italian diced tomatoes
1 (16 oz) jar/can Salsa or tomato sauce
1 (14.5 oz) chicken broth
1 c. Quaker Quick Barley
3 c. water
1 T. chili powder
1 tsp. cumin
1 (15 oz) can black beans, drained and rinsed
1 (15 oz) can corn, drained
1 ½ lbs boiled chicken breasts in chunks (can use food storage substitution, see chart)
Cheddar cheese, sour cream, tortilla chips (optional)

Directions:
In a large pot, combine the first 7 ingredients. Bring to a boil, cover and reduce heat to low. Simmer for 20 minutes, stirring occasionally. Meanwhile boil the chicken in a separate pan. Add beans, corn, and chicken to large pot. Cook on high until chili comes to a boil. Cover and reduce heat to low. Simmer for another 5-10 minutes or until barley is tender. If desired, top with shredded cheese, sour cream, and tortilla chips. Makes a huge batch!

Chocolate Cake

Ingredients:
3 c. sifted flour
2 c. sugar
2 tsp. baking soda
1 tsp. salt
⅓ c. dark chocolate cocoa powder
2 tsp. white vinegar
2 tsp. vanilla
¾ c. canola oil
2 c. water
Frosting ingredients (see below)

Directions:
Pre-heat oven to 350 degrees. Put all dry ingredients into a large bowl and sift together. Mix all the wet into one bowl then add to dry ingredients. This is a really wet batter and there may be a few lumps. Pour into a 13 x 9 un-greased pan. Bake for approximately 40 minutes at 350. (Reduce oven temperature to 325 degrees and increase cook time to 45 minutes for a glass pan).

Frosting:
Set aside 1 cup chocolate chips and 2 handfuls of marshmallows. In a sauce pan add: 1 cup sugar, ¼ cup butter, ¼ cup milk. Stir occasionally on a medium heat until it comes to a boil. Do not boil. Remove from burner. Stir in 1 cup chocolate chips and 2 handfuls of marshmallows until melted into frosting. Frost cake.

Chow Mein Casserole

Ingredients:
1 lb hamburger (can use food storage substitution, see chart)
½ an onion chopped (can use food storage substitution, see chart)
½ c. rice, cooked
2 cans cream of chicken soup (use bean flour substitution {found on page 149})
1 ½ c. hot water (if using bean flour substitution, skip the water)
⅛ c. soy sauce
¼ tsp. ground pepper
½ can chow mein noodles (about 3 oz)

Directions:
Preheat oven to 350°. Mix all ingredients together (except chow mein noodles). Bake in serving bowl covered with foil for 45 minutes. Take off cover. Pour 3 oz. (½ can) of chow mein noodles over top. Cook uncovered for 15 more minutes. Let set for 5-10 minutes after cooking to thicken.

Cookie Clay Dough

Ingredients:
½ c. sugar
½ c. brown sugar, firmly packed
½ c. butter (1 cube)
1 tsp. vanilla
1 egg (can use food storage substitution, see chart)
2 c. whole wheat flour
1 extra large egg (can use food storage substitution, see chart)
1 tsp. baking powder
½ tsp. salt
½ tsp. cinnamon

Directions:
Cream together first 5 ingredients with a mixer. In a separate bowl combine all dry ingredients. Slowly add to the creamy mixture until it reaches the consistency of Play-Doh. Give the Cookie Clay Dough to your kids and let them make shapes, letters out of it. They can use it like they would use regular Play-Doh. Once they are finished, put all of the shapes on a cookie sheet and bake at 350 degrees for 10-15 minutes. *Recipe from Everyday Food Storage

Corn Dog Muffins

Ingredients:
1 ½ c. cornmeal (about 1 c. fresh ground popcorn)
2 ½ c. flour (about 2 c. fresh ground wheat)
½ c. white sugar
¼ c. brown sugar
4 tsp. baking powder
1 tsp. salt
2 eggs (can use food storage substitution, see chart)
2 c. milk (can use food storage substitution, see chart)
8 oz. shredded cheddar cheese
6 hot dogs cut in thirds

Directions:
Preheat oven to 400 degrees. Mix dry ingredients in large bowl. Beat eggs and milk in a separate bowl. Add to dry mix and add cheese just until moistened. Spoon mixture into muffin tins until ⅔ full. Add 1 hot dog chunk to each muffin. Bake for 14-18 minutes or until golden brown.

Corncakes

Ingredients:
1 ¼ c. whole wheat flour
⅓ c. cornmeal (or fresh ground popcorn kernels)
1 egg (can use food storage substitution, see chart)
⅓ c. granulated sugar
1 ½ c. buttermilk {see powdered milk substitution found on page 140}
1 tsp. baking powder
1 tsp. baking soda
¼ c. vegetable oil
½ tsp. salt

Directions:
Preheat a skillet over medium heat. Spray skillet with nonstick spray. Combine all ingredients in a large bowl with a mixer set on medium speed. Mix until smooth, but don't over mix. Pour the batter by ¼ – ⅓ cup portions into the hot pan and cook for 1 to 3 minutes per side or until brown. Repeat with remaining batter.

Cream of Chicken Soup

Ingredients:
4 T. of any white bean, ground into 5 T. of bean flour
1 ¾ c. water
4 tsp. chicken bouillon

Directions:
Combine all ingredients and mix well. Cook on stovetop at medium temperature until thick and boiling. The soup should boil for 3 minutes to ensure that the beans get all the way cooked for safety reasons.

Creamy Potato Soup

Ingredients:
4 c. cubed potatoes (can use food storage substitution, see chart)
½ c. minced onions (can use food storage substitution, see chart)
2 tsp. salt
3 T. chicken bouillon
2 c. diced carrots (can use food storage substitution, see chart)
2 c. diced celery (can use food storage substitution, see chart)
10 oz frozen broccoli (can use food storage substitution, see chart)
1 T. dry mustard
4 T. white bean flour mixed with ¾ c. water (any white bean ground into flour)
Cheddar cheese for topping

Directions:
In one pot cover the potatoes and onions with water, and add the chicken bouillon and salt. In a different pot, put all the carrots, celery, and broccoli together with very little water and start cooking. If using freeze-dried veggies, add a little more water. Once the potatoes are done cooking and very soft, take a masher, and very LIGHTLY mash them. This will get the soup creamy without flour, butter, and milk. After the potatoes are slightly mashed, add the carrots, celery and broccoli. It will be a little liquidy still, add white bean flour/water mixture to thicken. Let boil for at least 3 minutes to get the beans cooked. Add the dry mustard. Top with cheddar cheese if desired.

Curried Lentils & Rice

Ingredients:
2 c. long-grain white rice
1 T. vegetable or canola oil
1 T. curry powder
½ tsp. onion powder
4 c. water
1 c. lentils (red or brown)
1 tsp. honey
1 T. balsamic vinegar
1 tsp. salt

Directions:
In one saucepan, cook rice according to package directions. In second large saucepan, heat oil & stir in curry powder & powdered onion. Heat the spiced oil mixture for 2 minutes while stirring. Add the 4 cups of water and lentils, stir & bring to boil. Cover and simmer for 20-25 minutes or until lentils are soft. Remove from heat and stir in the honey, balsamic vinegar & salt. Serve spooned over rice. May garnish with sour cream or salsa.

Enchilada Pie (Food Storage)

Ingredients:
1 ½ c. cooked black beans
¼ c. dehydrated onion
1 batch of cream of chicken soup from bean flour {recipe found on page 149}
4 oz can diced green chilies
8 oz can enchilada sauce
6 whole wheat tortillas {recipe found on page 169}
2 c. freeze-dried cheese
2 c. freeze-dried chicken

Directions:
Cook tortillas and black beans. Hydrate chicken and cheese (the measurements given are the ingredients dry) While chicken and cheese are hydrating make cream of chicken bean sauce. Add beans, onions, cream of chicken sauce, diced green chilies, enchilada sauce, and chicken in a large bowl. Place tortillas in greased 9 by 13 inch pan. Top with half the bean mixture and half the cheese. Repeat the layers. Bake at 350 degrees for 40 minutes. Cool slightly and cut in squares.

Enchilada Pie (Traditional Recipe)

Ingredients:
1 16 oz can black beans
1 lg onion
1 can cream of chicken soup
1 can cream of mushroom soup
¾ cup of milk
4 oz can diced green chilies
8 oz can mild enchilada sauce
1 pkg soft tortillas
½ lb cheddar cheese, grated
½ lb Monterrey jack cheese, grated
3 chicken breasts, cooked and shredded

Directions:
Wash and cook beans. Mix next 6 ingredients with beans. Place tortillas in greased 9 by 13 inch pan. Top with half the bean mixture and half the cheese. Repeat the layers. Bake at 350 degrees for 40 minutes. Cool slightly and cut in squares.

Ezekiel Bread

Ingredients:
2 ½ c. wheat berries
1 ¼ c. spelt
½ c. barley
½ c. millet
¼ c. dry green lentils
2 T. dry great northern beans
2 T. dry kidney beans
2 T. dried pinto beans
4 c. warm water
1 c. honey
½ c. olive oil
2 (¼ ounce) packages active dry yeast
2 tsp. salt

Directions:
Measure the water, honey, olive oil, and yeast into a large bowl. Let sit for 3 to 5 minutes. Stir all of the grains and beans together until well mixed. Grind in a grain mill. Add fresh milled flour and salt to the yeast mixture; stir until well mixed, about 10 minutes.

The dough will be like that of a batter bread. Pour dough into two greased 9 x 5 inch loaf pans. Let rise in a warm place for about 1 hour, or until dough has reached top of the pan. Bake at 350 degrees for 45 to 50 minutes, or until loaves are golden brown.

Grandma Lori's Sugar Cookies

Cookie Ingredients:
2 c. butter – room temp.
2 c. white sugar
2 eggs
2 tsp. vanilla
1 c. sour cream (no light or fat free)
6 c. white flour
2 tsp. baking soda
1 tsp. salt

Frosting Ingredients:
Ingredients:
½ c. butter
8 oz. cream cheese
1 tsp. vanilla
3 c. powdered sugar

Directions:
Beat the first 4 ingredients very well, then fold in sour cream. Add flour, soda and salt. This is quite a sticky dough, so you roll it out on a well-floured surface. Roll them a little thicker than normal cookies. Bake at 350 for 7-10 min. Do not overcook. Let cool, then place on wax paper. Frosting: Mix first 3 ingredients, then mix in powdered sugar.

Granola Bars

Ingredients:
4 ½ c. rolled oats
1 c. all-purpose flour (or whole wheat)
1 tsp. baking soda
1 tsp. vanilla extract
⅔ c. butter, softened
½ c. honey
⅓ c. packed brown sugar
2 c. miniature semisweet chocolate chips

Directions:
Lightly grease one 9×13 inch pan. In a large mixing bowl combine the oats, flour, baking soda, vanilla, butter or margarine, honey and brown sugar. Stir in the 2 cups assorted chocolate chips. Lightly press mixture into the prepared pan. Bake at 325 degrees for 18 to 22 minutes or until golden brown. Let cool for 10 minutes then cut into bars. Let bars cool completely in pan before removing or serving.

Greek Lentil Soup

Ingredients:
2 c. lentils, dried
4 c. cold water
1 c. onion,
1 clove garlic, crushed
4 c. beef broth
¼ tsp. black pepper
½ c. celery, chopped (can use food storage substitution, see chart)
2 c. stewed tomatoes
1 bay leaf
1 c. carrots (can use food storage substitution, see chart)
3 T. parsley, chopped (can use food storage substitution, see chart)
½ tsp. oregano (can use food storage substitution, see chart)
2 T. vinegar

Directions:
Wash lentils, drain well. Combine lentils with all ingredients except vinegar. Bring to a boil. Lower heat; cover and simmer 2 hours or until lentils are tender. Add vinegar and simmer 30 minutes more. Remove bay leaf. Serve soup.

Homemade Egg McMuffins

Instructions:
1 egg
1 T. egg white powder (equivalent to 3 egg whites)
2 T. water

Directions:
Mix and scramble egg, egg white powder, and water. Fry in pan. Use as the base for an Egg McMuffin by adding ham and cheese and putting on an English Muffin. It tastes the same as using real egg whites, but you don't waste as many yolks and you can still cut back on the fat and calories.

Homemade Hummus

Ingredients:
2 c. soaked chickpeas or 1 16 oz can beans, drained
¼ c. lemon juice
1 T. tahini (sesame seed oil)
2 cloves garlic or 2 tsp. garlic powder
1 tsp. curry powder
½ small jar of roasted red peppers, drained

Directions:
Mince the garlic, put in food processor. Add the garbanzo beans, puree. Add the oil and juice, puree again. Drain and add roasted red peppers, add curry, blend.
If the beans are soft, then you'll only have to process for a minute. When using soaked, but not cooked beans, process for five minutes or until smooth. Use as a spread or a dip.
*Recipe from Safely Gathered In

Homemade Mayonnaise

Ingredients:
1 T. powdered egg (heaping)
1 T. water
1 pinch of sugar
½ tsp. salt
1 T. lemon juice
½ tsp. mustard (any flavor you enjoy)
½ - ¾ c. oil

Directions:
Mix all the ingredients except the oil in a small blender, food processor, or in a bowl with a hand wand style blender. Add a few drops of oil and mix until well blended. Add a few more drops and mix until well blended. Keep adding drops very slowly with full mixing in between until mayonnaise thickens. This recipe makes a small batch as it only stores in the fridge 3-5 days. You can double or triple the recipe if you need more.

Homemade Pasta

Ingredients:
1 ½ c. semolina flour
1 ½ c. freshly ground whole wheat flour
½ tsp. salt
4 eggs
¼ c. water
¼ c. olive oil

Directions:
Combine semolina, wheat flour, and salt. Beat eggs lightly. Mix eggs, water and oil. Stir in to four mixture until a stiff dough forms. You may need to add a little more flour. Knead 10 minutes or until elastic. Let rest, covered for 20 minutes. Roll out thinly. Cut into desired shape or shape with machine. Cook in boiling, salted water for 2-5 minutes.

Homemade Ranch Dip or Dressing

Ingredients:
1 c. plain greek yogurt (full fat)
½ c. sour cream (can use food storage substitution, see chart)
½ tsp. garlic powder
½ tsp. dill
¼ tsp. pepper
3 T. minced fresh parsley (can use food storage substitution, see chart)
2 T. minced fresh chives (can use food storage substitution, see chart)
salt to taste

Directions:
Combine ingredients, and chill before serving. If using powdered sour cream, add ½ c. sour cream powder to the mixture, then add water slowly until you get desired texture.

Homemade Rice-A-Roni

Ingredients:
2 c. rice
1 c. angel hair, vermicelli or spaghettini pasta, broken into very small pieces
¼ c. parsley (can use food storage substitution, see chart)
6 T. chicken bouillon powder
2 tsp. onion powder
½ tsp. garlic powder
¼ tsp. thyme

Directions:
Combine all ingredients and mix well. To prepare: Melt 2 T. butter in a skillet. Add 1 c. of the mix and stir. Add 2 ¼ c. water. Bring to a boil. Reduce heat to low, cover and simmer for 15 minutes.

Homemade Smoothies

Ingredients:
¾ c. frozen strawberries (can use food storage substitution, see chart)
½ c. frozen blueberries (can use food storage substitution, see chart)
½ c. frozen peaches or raspberries (can use food storage substitution, see chart)
1 c. powdered milk, prepared
½ c. yogurt (frozen works great)
Sugar to taste, if desired

Directions:
Pour milk into blender. Add fruit, yogurt, and any other sweetener you desire.

Honey Whole Wheat Bread

Ingredients:
2 c. all-purpose flour
1 tsp. salt
1 pkg. quick rise yeast
¾ c. milk (can use food storage substitution, see chart)
¾ c. water
2 T. honey
2 T. vegetable oil
2 c. whole wheat flour

Directions:
Combine 1 ½ cups all-purpose flour, salt, and yeast in large mixing bowl. Heat milk, water, honey and oil until hot to touch. Gradually add to dry ingredients. Beat 2 minutes at medium speed of mixer, scraping bowl occasionally. Add ½ cup all-purpose flour. Beat at high speed for 2 minutes, scraping bowl occasionally. With spoon, stir in whole wheat flour and enough additional all-purpose flour to make stiff dough. Knead on lightly floured surface until smooth and elastic, about 6-8 minutes. Place in greased bowl, turning to grease top. Cover, let rest for 10 minutes. Spray loaf pan with vegetable pan spray. Roll dough to 12×8" rectangle. Roll up from short end to make loaf. Pinch seam and ends to seal. Place, seam side down, in prepared pan. Cover, let rise in warm place until doubled in size, about 30 minutes. Bake at 375° for 35 minutes or until bread sounds hollow when tapped. Remove from pan, cool in a wire rack.

Hot Fudge Sauce

Ingredients:
1 can evaporated milk {see powdered milk substitution found on page 140}
2 c. semisweet chocolate chips
½ c. sugar
1 T. butter or margarine
1 tsp. vanilla

Directions:
In a 2-quart sauce pan mix your evaporated milk with a whisk. Add chocolate chips and sugar and heat over medium heat, stirring constantly until it boils. Remove from heat and stir in butter and vanilla. Let cool for at least 30 minutes or until sauce begins to thicken. Serve warm. Store your remaining sauce covered in the refrigerator up to 4 weeks. Sauce becomes firm when refrigerated; heat slightly before serving (sauce will become thin if overheated). *Recipe from Everyday Food Storage

Meatballs Tetrazzini

Ingredients:
1 batch of basic meatballs {recipe found on page 142}
8 oz package spaghetti
1 can condensed tomato soup
¼ c. freeze-dried onion
½ tsp. salt
1 c. milk (can use food storage substitution, see chart)
⅛ tsp. pepper
8 oz shredded cheddar cheese (can use food storage substitution, see chart)

Directions:
Prepare basic meatball recipe. Preheat oven to 350 degrees. Cook spaghetti and drain. Combine soup, milk, onion, salt, pepper, and cheese. Heat until cheese is melted. Arrange meatballs and spaghetti in a 9×13 pan. Pour liquid mixture over meatballs and toss to mix well. Bake for 30 minutes until hot and serve immediately.

Mexican Casserole

Ingredients:
1 family size package Kraft macaroni and cheese
(or 3 c. macaroni, ½ c. powdered cheese, 6 tsp. butter, 6 tsp. of powdered milk)
½ lb. lean hamburger browned (can use food storage substitution, see chart)
½ onion, chopped (can use food storage substitution, see chart)
1 can chili with beans
1 can tomato soup
1 T. chili powder
1 can corn
Cheddar cheese, cubed (optional)
Fritos (optional)

Directions:
Preheat oven to 350°. Cook Kraft dinner according to directions in large pot. Meanwhile, brown hamburger with onion. Add to Kraft dinner with remaining ingredients. Heat through. Pour into casserole dish and top with Fritos. Cover and bake 30 minutes.

No-Bake Peanut Butter Energy Bites

Ingredients:
2 c. old fashion oats
½ c. peanut butter
⅓ c. raw honey
½ c. chocolate chips
1 tsp. vanilla

Directions:
Put all the ingredients in a bowl and mix. Put the mixture in the fridge for 30 minutes to cool. After the mixture is cool, roll into balls. Store in an airtight container in the fridge or freezer.

Patriotic Jello

Ingredients:
2 3 oz packages blue jello
2 3 oz packages strawberry jello
2 envelopes unflavored gelatin
14 oz can sweetened condensed Milk (can use food storage substitution, see chart)
Freeze-dried strawberries
Freeze-dried blueberries
Spiff-E-Whip (powdered whipped topping)

Directions:
Make your blue layer of jello. Mix 2 packages of blue jello with 2 cups of boiling water until dissolved. Then add 1 cup of ice cold water and stir. Pour into a 9×12 pan. Sprinkle freeze-dried blueberries evenly into the pan and stir them in so they are covered with liquid. Let set in fridge for 4 hours or overnight.
Make your white layer of jello. Sprinkle 2 envelopes of unflavored gelatin into ½ cup of cold water. After it thickens, add 1 ½ cups of boiling water and mix in until it dissolves. Stir in the can of sweetened condensed milk until smooth. Let cool (but don't leave it out too long) Pour over hardened blue layer. Let chill for 4 hours or overnight.
Make your red layer of jello. Mix 2 packages of blue jello with 2 cups of boiling water until dissolved. Then add 1 cup of ice cold water and stir. Sprinkle freeze-dried strawberries into the liquid. Pour entire mixture over top of white layer. Let set in fridge for 4 hours or overnight.
Once the red layer has set firmly, you can decorate the top with a flag if desired. Mix 1 cup of Spiff-E-Whip with 1 cup of ice water and beat with a mixer for about 3-4 minutes until it has a whipped cream consistency. While beating the whipped cream, reconstitute some freeze-dried blueberries and strawberries for the topping. Spread the whipped cream over top and decorate like a flag.

Pea Soup

Ingredients:
2½ T. of dried peas (green or yellow) ground to make 3 T. pea flour
1 ½ c. cold water
2 tsp. chicken bouillon

Directions:
Mix ½ c. cold water and 3 T. pea flour in a bowl, set aside. Bring 1 c. water and 2 tsp. of chicken bouillon to a boil. Add in pea mixture. Bring back to a boil. Soup will thicken. You can add shredded carrots, veggies, or onion powder. This makes a small batch of soup.

Peanut Butter Bread

Ingredients:
2 ½ c flour
3 tsp. baking powder
½ tsp. salt
⅔ c. sugar
⅓ c. instant nonfat dry milk
1 egg beaten (can use food storage substitution, see chart)
1 Tbsp. grated orange rind (or 1 tsp. orange flavoring)
¾ c. water
½ c. peanut butter

Directions:
Mix flour baking powder salt sugar dry milk and peanut butter into a bowl. Add the orange rind, then in a separate bowl combine the egg and water then add to the flour mixture. Stir until just mixed. Pour into a greased 9x5x3 loaf pan bake in a moderate oven at 350 degrees for 50 to 60 minutes remove from pan and cool on a wire rack

Pizza Casserole

Ingredients:
16 oz pkg. rotini pasta
2 c. freeze-dried sausage crumbles
½ c. freeze-dried green peppers
¾ c. tomato sauce powder
3 c. water
2-3 c. freeze-dried mozzarella cheese
1 small pkg. sliced pepperoni

Directions:
Preheat oven to 350 degrees. Lightly grease a 9X13 casserole dish. Cook rotini noodles until slightly underdone. While pasta is cooking, lightly brown the dried sausage crumbles (before reconstituting). Mix tomato sauce powder with water until smooth, add browned sausage and freeze-dried green peppers. They will rehydrate in the sauce so no need to do that beforehand. Combine the sauce and the noodles and pour into the casserole dish. Lay freeze-dried cheese out on a plate covered with a paper towel. Spray it with water using a spray bottle until the cheese is fully hydrated and not crunchy any more. Sprinkle over the top of the noodle/sauce mixture. Top with pepperoni slices. Bake 20-25 minutes in the oven.

Poppyseed Chicken (Food Storage)

Ingredients:
1 qt jar home-canned chicken or use 3 c. freeze-dried chicken reconstituted
2 cans cream of chicken soup
1 ½ c. sour cream powder, rehydrated with ¾ c. water
½ c. butter powder, rehydrated with ½ c. water

Topping:
½ c. butter powder, rehydrated with ½ cup water
2 tubes ritz crackers, crushed
2 T. poppyseeds

Directions:
Combine cream of chicken soup, sour cream, and butter. Pour over chicken in a 9×13 pan or a slightly smaller oval casserole dish. Combine topping ingredients in small bowl. Use your hands to sprinkle evenly over top of chicken mixture. Bake at 350 degrees for 20-30 minutes or until heated through. Cover with foil until the last 5 minutes or the topping may get browner than you like. Serve over rotini noodles. While the topping does work with butter powder it is easier and turns out better just using melted butter.

Poppyseed Chicken (Traditional Recipe)

Ingredients:
1 ½ pounds chicken, diced and boiled
2 cans cream of chicken soup
12-16 oz sour cream
½ c. melted butter

Topping:
½ cup melted butter
2 tubes ritz crackers, crushed
2 T. poppyseeds

Directions:
Combine cream of chicken soup, sour cream, and butter. Pour over cooked chicken in a 9×13 pan or a slightly smaller oval casserole dish. Combine topping ingredients in small bowl. Sprinkle over top of chicken mixture. Bake at 350 degrees for 20-30 minutes or until heated through. Cover with foil until the last 5 minutes. Serve over rotini noodles.

Real Chili Beans

Ingredients:
1 lb. lean hamburger (can use food storage substitution, see chart)
2 c. dried pinto beans
8 oz. can of tomato sauce
1 lb stewed tomatoes
2 T. oil
1 onion, chopped (can use food storage substitution, see chart)
1 clove of garlic, finely chopped
2 tsp. salt
¼ tsp. paprika
1 ½ tsp. ground cumin
1 T. oregano
1 pinch chili pepper flakes
3 T. chili powder
⅛ tsp. cayenne pepper

Directions:
Soak beans overnight. Drain and cover with fresh water. Bring to a boil and simmer for 2 hours. Drain and add to crock-pot. Sauté the chopped onion and garlic in oil until limp. Stir in all seasonings. Add tomatoes and sauce and simmer for 20 minutes. Brown beef in small fry pan. Drain and add to crock-pot. Add the tomato/seasoning mixture that was simmering plus 5 cups of hot water to crock-pot. Simmer in crock-pot at least 7 hours.

Rice Pudding

Ingredients:
2 eggs, beaten (can use food storage substitution, see chart)
½ c. sugar
¼ tsp. salt
2 c. milk (can use food storage substitution, see chart)
1 ¼ c. cooked white rice, cooled (leftovers work great)
½ c. raisins (optional)
Cinnamon and Nutmeg to taste

Directions:
Preheat oven to 325 degrees. Mix all the ingredients together and pour into a greased 1 qt. bowl. Set the bowl in a shallow pan. Pour hot water into the pan about 1 inch deep. Put pan into the oven and bake for 1 ½ hours.

Salsa, Chicken, and Black Bean Soup

Ingredients:
2 c. freeze-dried chicken
1 ½ c. instant black beans or 16 oz canned black beans
1 c. freeze-dried corn
4 ½ c. chicken broth (or water with bouillon)
12-16 oz. salsa
1 ½ tsp. cumin

Directions:
Add chicken, instant beans, and corn to a pot. Pour the chicken broth over top and stir everything in. If using more fresh foods than freeze-dried you can reduce the broth to only 4 cups. Stir in salsa and cumin. Bring to a boil then simmer for 20 mins.

Sugar Bars

Crust:
1 c. butter
½ c. powdered sugar
½ tsp. salt
2 c. flour

Filling Sugar:
2 eggs (can use food storage substitution, see chart)
2 c. brown sugar
2 T. vinegar
½ c. melted butter (can use food storage substitution, see chart)

Directions:
Spread crust in two 9 x 13 pans. Mix filling and place on top of crust. Bake at 350 for 30 to 40 minutes. Enjoy a delicious treat for your birthday or any other time!

Super Cherry Pie

Ingredients:
Pie shell, uncooked
⅓ c. slivered almonds – press into pie shell before baking, then bake
1 c. sweetened condensed milk {see recipe found on page 166}
1 tsp. vanilla
½ c. cream, whipped
⅓ c. lemon juice
½ tsp. almond extract
1 can of cherry pie filling

Directions:
Mix together milk, vanilla, whipped cream, lemon juice, and almond extract in the order listed. Pour into baked pie shell with almonds pressed into it. Top with 1 can of cherry pie filling. Refrigerate 3 hours or longer.

Sweetened Condensed Milk

Ingredients:
½ c. hot water
1 c. powdered milk
1 c. sugar
1 T. butter

Directions:
Blend in blender very well. Can be stored in the refrigerator or frozen. Makes equivalent of 14 oz can.

Tortellini Chicken Soup

Ingredients:
12.5 oz can chicken (can use food storage substitution, see chart)
¼ c. dehydrated celery
2 T. dehydrated onions
2 ½ c. water
8 c. chicken broth (or water mixed with chicken bouillon)
½ tsp. celery seed
½ tsp. basil
½ tsp. garlic salt
1 tsp. salt
Sprinkle of red pepper flakes (optional)
12 oz package of Barilla Tortellini (the shelf stable variety)

Directions:
Bring the water and chicken broth to a boil. Add spices. Add chicken (cut it up small if you like smaller chunks). Add dehydrated celery and onions. Add tortellini after it returns to a boil. Cook according to your package directions (probably about 10-12 minutes).

White Sauce Mac 'N' Cheese (Powdered Milk)

Ingredients:
1 lb macaroni noodles
¼ c. butter
¼ c. flour
1 c. water mixed with 3 T. powdered milk
1 tsp. seasoned salt
Cheese cubes (optional)
Ham cubes (optional)

Directions:
Cook noodles according to package directions. Drain and set aside. Melt butter in large saucepan. Whisk in the flour until smooth. Slowly stir in reconstituted milk until well mixed in. Add seasoned salt. Let cook for a little while until it starts to thicken. Add in the macaroni noodles. Add in a little more milk if it seems too thick. Can add more seasoned salt according to taste. Add ham and cheese cubes right before serving.

White Sauce Mac 'N' Cheese (Legumes)

Ingredients:
3 c. macaroni noodles
4 T. any white bean, ground into 5 T. of bean flour
1 c. water
¾ c. milk (can use food storage substitution, see chart)
2 tsp. seasoned salt
Cheese cubes (optional)
Ham cubes (optional)

Directions:
Cook noodles according to package directions. Drain and set aside. Grind ¼ cup of white beans in your wheat grinder to make about 5 T. of bean flour. Put 1 cup of water in large saucepan. Slowly whisk in ground bean flour. Continue to whisk frequently until starts to thicken and bubble. Slowly stir in milk until it's a nice thick liquid consistency. Add seasoned salt (the bean version tends to need more than the flour/butter version). Add in the macaroni noodles. Add in a little more milk if it seems too thick. Add ham and cheese cubes right before serving.

Whole Wheat Pizza Dough

Ingredients:
2 ½ c. medium hot water
5 tsp. SAF instant yeast
2 T. sugar
3 T. oil
1 tsp. salt
6 c. flour (you can do half all-purpose and half wheat or 100% whole wheat)
½ cube of butter

Directions:
Pour medium hot water in mixing bowl. Sprinkle yeast on top and allow to dissolve. Add sugar, salt, and oil. Gradually add approximately 6 cups of flour. Use about ⅔ of the dough for pizza. Use the other ⅓ for breadsticks. Melt ½ cube of butter on cookie sheet in oven as it is heating to 400 degrees and melt in oven. Place dough on cookie sheet and press to fill pan, make sure butter gets on top of the dough. Add your sauce, cheese, and toppings. Cook for 10 to 12 minutes or until cheese is slightly browned and the crust is firm.

Whole Wheat Pumpkin Cake

Ingredients:
4 eggs (can use food storage substitution, see chart)
1 ⅔ c sugar
1 c. cooking oil
1 large can pumpkin
2 c. flour (whole wheat works great)
2 tsp. baking powder
2 tsp. cinnamon
1 tsp salt
1 tsp. soda

Frosting:
8 oz cream cheese
¾ c. butter
1 ½ tsp. vanilla
3 c. powdered sugar

Directions:
Preheat oven to 350°. Beat eggs, sugar, oil, and pumpkin. Stir in dry ingredients. Mix well. Bake for 30-35 minutes in a 9×13 ungreased pan. Mix together frosting ingredients and pour on top.

Whole Wheat Tortillas

Ingredients:
3 c. whole wheat flour
½ tsp. baking powder
1 tsp. salt
1 c. warm water
⅓ c. cooking oil

Directions:
Mix all dry ingredients together. Add the oil, then the water. Knead 5 minutes. Roll the dough out so you can easily make equal pieces. Let dough rest 10 minutes. Form into 12 balls. Roll thin (use pam spray if needed). Grill on both sides in a frying pan. They cook quickly (no need to grease the frying pan).

Wonderflour

Ingredients:
2 c. brown rice
2 c. pearled barley
2 c. spelt

Directions
Grind all 6 cups of grain in a grain mill. Use as a white flour replacement in most baked goods except yeast breads. Add about ½ cup extra flour per 3 cups of white flour used in recipes. *Recipe from Chef Brad

Worms and Dirt Pudding Treat

Instructions:
1 box chocolate pudding
Powdered milk
Water
Gummy worms

Directions:
Make chocolate pudding with powdered milk according to box instructions. Top with gummy worms. This is great for kids.

Made in the USA
Columbia, SC
16 August 2021